I0440033

So I Can See the Trees

Travels in the Maine North Woods and Baxter Park

TOD CHENEY

The Cabin Press

So I Can See the Trees:
Travels in the Maine North Woods and Baxter Park
Copyright ©2012 by Tod Cheney

All rights reserved. No part of this book may be reproduced in any form or by any electronic or mechanical means, including information storage and retrieval systems, without permission in writing from the author, except by a reviewer, who may quote brief passages in review.

Published by Cabin Press, 716 Range Road, Blue Hill, Maine 04614
Cover photograph copyright 2012 by Tod Cheney

Available as an ebook on Amazon Kindle

ISBN-13: 978-1482534887
ISBN-10: 1482534886

Manufactured in the United States of America

CONTENTS

PREFACE

The writing in this little book is my attempt to share my love of the Maine woods. I find the forests of northern Maine to be beautiful and exotic places—rich with metaphors for human life and living. When I am alone in the woods, I feel alert and connected to plants and animals, even while I am sometimes uncomfortable and even fearful.

In the Maine woods, the natural world hangs out in the open, in contrast to, say, any place where humans are settled. In many of these places, our cultural practices disguise, hide, or transform nature into something that is more refined, less threatening, or in some way more suitable to our comfort level. We don't like things too untamed or mysterious. The Maine woods are not immune to these alterations—but there are places where human impact is minimal.

Most of the Maine woods is owned by corporations and small private property owners. As far as my experience goes, these owners are generous extenders of a long tradition of public access. While there are a few sporting camps and private camps where access is restricted, most of the woods and waters are open to anyone who wants to go there and pay the fee (in season). In that sense, accessibility is similar to a national park, though both Baxter State Park and the Allagash Wilderness Waterway are controlled by the State of Maine. Particularly in the eastern part of the country, where so much land is gated and posted, this democratic and egalitarian model is something to be respected and honored.

I want to state that I am not an expert on any of the subjects broached in this book. I have no professional credentials for writing about the natural world, nor am I a guide of any kind, or especially expert in wilderness skills of hiking, canoeing, cooking, or camping. I have a modest measure of experience with these activities and mostly have found my own way, for better or worse. No practices or methods

1

related here should be construed as advice or recommendation of any kind. If someone learns something from my mistakes, fine.

Not long ago my mother endured a stay in the intensive care unit of a hospital where she was not able to see outside for several days. When my brother and I picked her up, we had to help her stand up from the wheelchair, take a couple of steps to the car, and ease her down into the front seat. As we started driving to the convalescent home, she said something that made a big impression on me.

"Let's go the long way, so I can see the trees."

There are probably lots of ways my mother and I differ in our orientation to trees, but the way she said that, I knew we agreed about one thing—that trees and nature are essential to the human heart.

Tod Cheney
Blue Hill, Maine
October, 2012

Chandler Pond—Winter Comes to the Woods

It's December and very cold. Holly and I are walking on the Pinkham Road, a logging highway that trends southwest toward Chamberlain Lake from Ashland. Maybe it's five degrees, and the wind feels like it's been tempered by Arctic ice. This is not the weather we hoped for when we booked the cabin a month ago. Temperatures then were hanging in the 60s. There was no ice anywhere in Maine. I'd imagined the weather holding, paddling a canoe on the pond, hiking into Big Reed Forest, the largest old growth forest remnant in New England—five thousand acres of woods that's never seen an ax under the protection of the Nature Conservancy, and only a few miles from our camp. In good weather we could walk to Big Reed.

"Hear that?" I ask.

"I hear the wind."

"There's wind, and something else."

"What?"

"Something's coming."

"What's that?"

"Don't know. It comes and goes."

"You're hearing the wind."

"There it is again. It's trucks."

It's a couple more minutes before three log carriers, so huge they're not road legal anywhere else, roar by us spraying clouds of snow, gravel, and diesel exhaust. The first two trucks slow as they pass, and we see the drivers talking on radios, but they gear up again and whoosh away down this outback road in the middle of the Maine woods. The third truck pulls to a stop a hundred yards ahead, then backs up.

"Are you guys all right?" the driver asks with a bemused smile. That's how unusual it is to see anyone walking on this road, no matter the time of year. It's a good question, and it's a good feeling this guy stopped.

"We're fine. Just out for a walk."

"Going for a long walk then?" He smiles again. He's sitting about twelve feet off the ground. The nearest town is fifty miles away.

"We're staying in a cabin near here."

"OK then."

"Thanks for stopping." We are all three smiling like we do agree it's unusual to be out walking on a logging road in December with wind chill south of zero. Not what most folks do for recreation.

"Look at those wheel nuts," says Holly as the truck rolls away. The top of the wheel is head high, and the chrome lugs stick out three inches from the rim. These rigs are the chariots of the North Country. You don't mess with these machines on their roads. That's what those wheel lugs are saying. Driving in yesterday, we passed these same trucks, and one had a skewed log sticking eight feet into our side of the road.

"It's nice to know they'll stop," I say as the sights and sounds of the logging truck fade into the wind.

Holly and I are close followers of the weather at all times of the year, but leading up to this trip I paid especially close attention. Weather would be a major factor. Camp utilities consist of a wood stove and a spring—"keep going past the outhouse to find it"—and a long driveway that would not be plowed if it snowed. Holly has expressed skepticism about middle-of-the-night trips to the outhouse in the snow. Despite the long lead-in of pleasant fall weather, the forecast was not good. Winter took control the day before we left home, and a nor'easter dropped eight inches across the north. The wind's supposed to blow like stink for three days. Temperatures in the low single numbers at night, and daytime highs around fifteen.

"Do you want to change our plans?" I asked on Tuesday. We were planning to leave Thursday.

"We've paid. We've set this time aside for the trip."

Right. I wonder if I'm turning into a wimp. A little cold and snow giving me second thoughts about a weekend in the woods?

We had to shovel out the snowplow's drift at the edge of the Pinkham Road to get in the driveway, and I'd say the eight inches on the ground is right at our comfort level in terms of getting out.

"It's a long way to shovel," Holly remarks as we get out of the car and look back at the slight upward grade of the driveway we've just come down. We have brought our own snow shovel as the owner advised. One of his messages stated that this cabin was not often used in the winter.

We get our stuff inside and get a fire going right off. It's a large cabin with plenty of space to spread out, and it looks pretty snug. I have walked into North Woods cabins in winter and seen daylight between every course of logs. I've stayed in others where snow blows across the floor. The stove in this one is old and little shaky, an Ashley that qualifies for antique status, not usually a desirable attribute for a wood stove, but it does put out heat and our prospects for staying warm look good. I shovel a path to the outhouse about a hundred feet away. The spring is frozen as predicted. Actually it's the black pipe running from the spring that's frozen, a clear spout of ice sticking out the end like the curve of a candy cane. The spring itself, farther back in the woods, is not frozen but not very accessible. We have brought drinking water from home anyway. Other water we will haul from the pond. With the Ashley slowing raising the temperature inside the cabin and confidence building that we are not going to burn the structure down, we set out on our first exploration to the main road and beyond.

After meeting the trucks about a mile east of the cabin's driveway, we head down one of the unplowed side roads. We see deer scrapes on young maples, and a few wind-sculpted white pines tower over what's left of the logged-out woods. We pass a side road posted with a "Project Notification" sign. The Seven Islands Land Company is the contractor, and part of the information on the sign includes GPS coordinates of the plot.

"They put that on everything now," says Holly. "They put GPS points on a septic system permit."

Hmm. And they guide bombs with GPS, too, I think. Someone could be watching us walk down this road through a satellite's eye and use GPS to steer a drone this way and blow us up, if they were so inclined. Just a little target practice, who's to know? What if we were terrorists crossing the Canadian border and working our way through safe houses to get to somewhere important, somewhere not in the middle of nowhere? Such is the character of wilderness these days. Whatever else, it is infinitely mappable, every square foot capable of being abstracted into coordinates.

Somewhere off to our right is Big Reed. There's a Big Reed Pond and a Little Reed Pond and a Reed Brook, and lying north of these waters is Reed Mountain. I am not sure if the forest we can see over in that direction is part of the Big Reed Preserve or not, but trudging a mile through the snow on the Connector Road has tired us, and the goal of reaching the old-growth forest on this trip begins to fade as the warm cabin beckons. We decide to return to the Pinkham Road and now walk headfirst into the wind. All the road signs have been shot up. That is, all the corporations' signs are full of holes. The signs belonging to the sporting camps have been left alone.

The cabin sits high on a knoll overlooking frozen Chandler Pond. In my mind's eye, I see calm blue-black water early in the morning and a wood canvas canoe floating on it like a duck. What I really see is yesterday's snow drifted over three to four inches of ice, maybe more in some places and less in others. These are not good conditions. The ice is not reliable anywhere, and the snow cover insulates the ice and keeps it from thickening up. This puts most of the pond out of bounds, as well as the regions around it which would have been accessible with either thicker ice or no ice at all. A snow-covered canoe sits on a couple of saw horses near the pond's edge.

Standing at the end of the dock, I chop a hole in the ice, and the thick pond water wells up and spreads over the ice. It's only two feet deep. We dip the pails, fill them, and carry fifteen gallons of water up the hill. No need to skimp on water when there's a pond full. During the climb to the cabin, lugging a sloshing pail of freezing cold water, is when I first think about taking a shower. I'm not sure how I'll do it yet, but I'm not in a hurry.

The environment and our own habits determine our routine. My bedtime and rising hours tend to coincide with darkness and daylight, which means in winter I am challenged to stay awake after 8 P.M. Rising time might be 4-4:30 A.M. The cabin has four beds, none big enough for the two of us to get a night's sleep, so we stake out individual quarters on the two widest beds which happen to be at opposite ends of the room. My bed is beneath a window, so I can look out at the silhouettes of spruces at the edge of the clearing, and if they are out, the yellow- white stars beyond.

We have gotten the temperature inside up to 65 degrees, plenty respectable, and it is not overly drafty, though as usual in an un-insulated building, you have to watch your backside. My front feels like 70, the back side of my chair, an almost comfortable Adirondack design I've pulled in from the porch, is more like 55. But the cabin is toasty enough that when we go to bed, I can leave the zipper on my sleeping bag open.

Breakfast is a considerable affair of thick-cut bacon, home fries, fried eggs, toast, and orange juice. And more coffee. We are in no hurry to go anywhere. It's five degrees out there, and there's nothing timid about the northerly gale. Not weather for a sauntering exploration in the woods. We complete the chores with thoroughness and deliberation. Fetching water is the most demanding. I suit up and carry an ax and steel pails down to the pond. The water hole freezes over in a couple hours, and overnight four inches of new ice has formed. The ax sends slivers of ice everywhere, so I chop with my eyes closed. It doesn't take long to hack out a hole large enough to dip the pail into. It's impossible to keep the tendrils of green weed out of the bucket, but it's not drinking water anyway. Five gallons of water times eight pounds per gallon makes forty sloshing pounds to carry up the snow covered bank. Three pails are plenty to get through the day. We keep a pail on the Ashley, and if we need to, we boost it a few more degrees on the gas stove, so there's no shortage of hot water. We fill the wood box from the wood shed, sweep the floor, and even up the piles of magazines and books and maps.

"OK, I'm ready to go out now," says Holly. It's after 10:30 A.M.

"Let's stay close by in the woods. The wind won't be so bad."

"Let's go up to that clearing alongside the driveway. That looks like we could get around OK there."

From the cabin road past the clearing, there is a large pine back in the woods that calls us in. Large pines have always been beacons in the woods. They have been sought out and chopped down almost as soon as the white man landed here. First for the king's navy masts, then for colonists' houses—for siding, doors, cabinets, floors, and furniture. Always men had a higher use for the pine trees than the tree's usefulness to itself. The voices in the wilderness howled for profits. One hundred and fifty years ago, writers observing Maine's forests already noted the bygone pine. We can only wonder what they must have been like, those stands of trees five, six feet across at the butt. The tree we head for today stands tall over its brethren, but it's only a child of a tree compared to the extinct king pines.

We descend from the cabin road through an old clearing. There are small pines head-high, and fresh deer tracks in the snow.

"They took gravel out of here. This is an old pit, probably for the camp road. Before the Pinkham Road, you had to fly into this camp. Some of them are still that way." There is a rim of excavation around us. The bank is too steep to climb up and the woods on top too thick to walk through.

"Let's go around this way, it's flatter."

"This looks like water."

"It is water, or ice."

"I'm not going over that."

"There, I went over it. If it holds me it'll hold you."

"I don't like that sound."

"It's not deep anyway."

We see lots of beaver sign. They have felled half a dozen trees six to eight inches in diameter. A couple got hung up, leaving the beavers' food out of reach. A lot of work for nothing. I wonder if a beaver gets pissed off when that happens, but doubt that anger is a beaver emotion. We work our way around the end of the excavation's berm to a more open flat area. There is a muffled gurgle of running water.

"Look. There's a dam. We're standing on a beaver pond."

"And there's the house."

"Where?"

"Right in front of you."

A little more surveillance reveals a dam stretching a couple of hundred feet that we can see, in a shallow crescent—starting somewhere over near the pine tree that had called us in here in the first place, and disappearing over on our left somewhere in the brush. We edge around, looking for the end of the dam which tapers down as the ground rises slightly. The cracking ice and running water have switched on Holly's common sense, and she stops and waits for me to fall in. A few steps later, I do crash through and am standing up to my knees in water beside the dome of ice that had supported me seconds before. About an inch of ice curves over a cavern of air. When I try to step back on top of the ice, it crumbles. After a couple of steps, I grab a small fir tree and pull myself on top of the dam. Somehow all that took only seconds, and the water did not go over the top of my boots.

"I knew that was going to happen."

"I know you did. So did I." And that was enough luck for one cold day. We did not make it to the pine tree.

We have been in the woods three days, and it is time for a shower. While five gallons of pond water warms on the wood stove, I develop a plan. This isn't going to be any sponge bath.

"Sure you don't want to join me?"

"I'm sure."

"It's not what you think."

"I'll pass."

When the water is ready, I carry it outside on the porch, strip quickly, and start pouring water over my head using a small ladle. The thermometer says eight degrees, and the air is calm and dark. The idea is to try and cover as much skin as possible with each pour. A third hand would help, but if you keep moving, it's a good system. The best part comes when I'm cleaned up, most of the soap is rinsed off, and there's still two and a half gallons of hot water. This time I pick up the bucket and pour all the water over my head. Wonderful. In a few minutes I'm wearing clean long underwear, clean socks, and sitting next to the fire with a glass of wine.

"Really, it's not what you'd expect. You don't get cold with all that hot water. You should give it a try."

"I'll stay with my own system, thank you."

"OK, I'm ready to see a moose any time."

"OK, I'm ready too."

The Maine woods evokes moose more than any other animal and fertilize our minds with images and expectations. Driving in the North Woods, one expects to see a moose around every bend in the road. Their long legs and caricature-like physiques fascinate us. The hairy rubber smirk of a mouth designed for dining at the bottom of shallow ponds suggests the moose knows something we don't, and the large horny antlers impress both girl moose and humans alike. I know of several humans who haunt the moose forests looking for shed antlers.

Well, we do not see any moose this trip. Not a track. Indeed, the weather seems to have laid low all wildlife, but finally on Sunday the wind dies down, and we begin to hear the woods. The frozen trees creak, a woodpecker drums a hollow log. The pond ice reports compressions and contractions. Pressure cracks fly like lightening north to south, searing the air with bolts of sound. Then, out of the vast forest, a squad of Canada Jays comes calling and looking for a bite to eat. These birds are well known for their gregariousness and visiting camps—a practice that brings them their rewards—in our case, several slabs of pita bread thrown onto the wood shed roof. A blue jay surprises us, showing up for a stake in the pita scraps, but he has to wait in line for the Canada Jays to finish. If he tries to cut in, the Canada Jays chase him out.

The cold has firmed up the ice enough that I take an early morning walk down the pond. I stay close to shore, as did a coyote sometime in the past couple of days. An ancient pine a few feet from shore draws me into the woods, and once more I crash through into a foot of water. The heat of the land retards formation of the ice, and I'd been walking on a snow bridge. Several pines along here are real old—three hundred, three hundred and fifty years probably. The old growth forest is right in front of me. Around the end of the little peninsula our cabin sits on, I come upon otter slides in the snow. One, two, three running steps, then a belly slide seven feet long. Then one, two, three steps again and another seven-foot slide. What are they doing? Is it all in fun, or is there a more serious side to the sliding?

I make a course twenty feet from shore, now and then testing the ice with a stick. Scattered throughout the blanket of snow are patches of translucent ice black as a north night sky. These places froze after the snowstorm, and at first they make me nervous. This ice is new, not insulated from the cold of the past four days, and so it is thickening faster than the snow ice. I prod the ice with my stick and stamp my foot. It doesn't budge the dark ice eyes of the pond. Locked into the surface of these dark eyes are dozens of tiny beaver sticks. The beaver must have dined at these spots just before freeze-up.

The sun shines brightly on the surface of the pond. It is pleasant on the ice, and for a few minutes I unzip my jacket to keep from sweating. After three days the wind has died away, and the air is calm. The forest sounds like an orchestra tuning—the woodpecker strums, the frozen trees inhale, a raven rasps a raw note. Then, out of nowhere, a pressure crack starts at the head of the pond and heads south so loud, sharp, and fast that I gasp for breath, as if it had stolen the air.

Allagash Lake—Alone on a Lake Gem

I have heard all these things about Allagash Lake. Allagash Lake is the jewel of the North Woods. Allagash Lake is a gem. Allagash Lake is hard to get to, the most remote of all Maine Lakes. There is no motorized transport allowed on Allagash Lake. "You've got to check out Allagash Lake," said an acquaintance who lives in the North Woods.

I remember the first time I saw the lake. It was raining that day in May, the air was mist, and the budding leaves spread through the woods like green fog. The ground squirted like a clam flat under my boots. Coming up on the lake through the forest, I saw the water gleam through the trees like pewter in candlelight. I came out of a nave of hemlock and stood before the miles of water spreading northwards. The water nuzzled the ledges. Far down the lake, water and sky dissolved into each other. Ice out was a recent event. All the earth was cool, and sleety droplets hung in the air like memories of winter. Daylight, already muted by the overcast, declined early in the afternoon, and the forest shadows urged me back home.

It took five months to return to Allagash Lake, this time with a canoe. During that time I spent a good amount of time musing over the "hard to get to" part and tried to decide the best way to go in. I had seen the Carry Trail, the mile-long section of an old loggers' tote road, now grass-covered with a few rocky washes where drainage flows across the top. I never considered portaging the traditional way with the canoe upside down on top of my head, nor did I have a canoe cart or any desire to buy one. The other route into the lake is to drive to Johnson Pond, paddle across the pond, and proceed down Johnson Stream for two miles to Allagash Stream which lets into the west end of the lake. The problem with that route is that, in an average September, there's not enough water in Johnson Steam to float a match, and you can pretty much count on dragging your canoe through a trench of muck. A friend who did it all advised the Carry, so that settled it. That meant I'd need wheels for the canoe, and I made it into a challenge. I would build a canoe carrier, but it was not going to cost any money.

I start doing drive-bys at the transfer station, looking for wheels in the metal pile. Right away a couple of kids' bikes turn up, and one has nice fat knobby tires that look like they would roll a canoe a few miles. I get out of the car and walk closer to the bikes leaning on a rusty furnace. I recall how bike wheels are specialized. They have their own integral little axles that set into forks of the bike frame, and unless you have a machine shop, they aren't easily adapted to other uses. I hesitate to take it home because I am not sure of a design. Then a car horn blows.

I look up and see a blue van idling behind my Pathfinder. I walk around to the driver's side of my car and see there's plenty of room for a vehicle to get by. The guy in the van can drive by and dump his load with no inconvenience or danger to himself. In thirty years I'd never heard a horn blow at the transfer station. I wave him through and turn to open my car door to get in. I have one leg up on the floor when he guns his engine and careens past only inches away.

"Hey, what's your problem?" I yell.He jumps out of his van and runs around to the back and pulls on an old washing machine.

"No picking! That's what the sign says. No picking!" he screams. The veins in his neck are bulging. He drops the washer onto the ground, storms back to the drivers seat, and spins out around the u-turn at the end of the metal pile. I drive home, congratulating myself I didn't do anything to escalate the incident, but also berating myself for not telling the asshole to go back where he came from. You can't win those situations.

A few days later, I go by the dump again and check to see if the bike is still there. It is and I bring it home and remove the wheels. I still don't know what to do, but sometimes getting started makes the ideas come. Upon loosening the nuts on one wheel, I confirm the ball bearings packed inside like peas in a pod are going to scatter if I go further, so I tighten it back up. Then comes the brainstorm of replicating the function of the bike forks using scrap plywood. No need to tinker with the wheel assemblies after all.

I make two forks. Each uses two pieces of 3/8" plywood about 18" square. They are screwed to a piece of 2 x 4 18" long, and the wheel is fitted into holes drilled through the plywood fork. The two forks are screwed to a 5/8" plywood platform where the canoe will sit. It's like a two-wheeled unicycle, and getting the canoe on top of a cart that wants to be lying down proves something like a Houdini act; but once it's on and tied, I can move the canoe around the shop floor with deceptive ease. I might want to test drive the rig on the ground later, but the basic design looks like it's up to the task.

Even after building the cart, I have second thoughts about getting to the lake via the Carry Trail. It's hard to discard the concept of driving the canoe and gear to water's edge in favor of pushing it overland for a mile. In the weeks leading up to the trip, I visit the canoe and cart in the shed many times. Piece by piece, I take gear down there, put it in the canoe, and push it around on the floor. There's the new wangan which holds the "camp kitchen" (already determined to be too big), the forty-year- old Coleman cooler, the ax, bow saw, tent, sleeping pad, tarps, ropes, paddle, and pole—and the canoe still rolls easily with one hand—on the shop floor.

I watch the weather through the last two weeks of September. The third week looks good, but a couple of appointments force me to push the trip back, and as a string of pleasant fall days slips by, I watch the forecast stretch out into a solid week of showers and rain.

For this trip I decide to drive in from the Millinocket side. First stop is Two Rivers Canoe and Tackle in Medway for some fall flies. I have not been much of a fisherman for a long time, but I've been wetting a little line to see if my interest rekindles and makes me more enthusiastic. The poetry of fishing attracts me, but fish flesh stuck on a hook is not a happy situation for anyone, and so there is a push and pull—like there is for so many things in life.

"I'm looking to get a few flies," I say to a man standing behind the fly cases.

"I heard that," says Barry, the owner of the store who stands several feet away. In an instant he is beside a wooden fly case holding a specimen between his thumb and forefinger before me as if I were a trout.

"It's red this time of year. You want something red," says Barry. "Like this here, the Montreal Whore."

"OK. I'll take one of those.

"And this one here, a Moby Dick...this one has a brownish wing..."

"Wait, I want to write these down. Now this one was..."

"Montreal Whore, you'll remember that one. And a Moby Dick..."

"OK."

"And this one here, also red with a sort of orange head, Muddler Hornby. Yup, red is what's working for me this time of year, around the ponds here."

I write the fly names down on the back page of a September *Northwoods Sporting Journal*. There's a big bull moose on the cover. "Surefire Moose Tactics" is the feature story, which reminds me I've forgotten to pack hunter orange. I pick out an orange hat to go with my Montreal Whore.

The last stop before there's nothing left to stop for—at least that you can buy—is the Katahdin Store at the side of the Golden Road where Millinocket Lake and Ambejejus Lake come together, where the sign out on the road says, "200 Cases of Cold Beer." They sell the usual tourist schlock in trade—moose t-shirts, Katahdin caps, moose mugs. They sell the standard American fare of chips, soda, candy, cigarettes, and cold beer. I stop for two things: something more solid than coffee for my stomach and, if possible, something to read, because this is an unusual little store. Out behind the chips and candy and cases of beer, like an oasis in a desert, is a room full of books. Here, displayed on nice wood shelves, are many classic titles of North Woods literature. It's like walking into a roomful of friends. *Lost on a Mountain in Maine. Nine Mile Bridge. We Took to the Woods.* Guidebooks for Baxter, Katahdin country, and the Appalachian Trail. *The Maine Woods.* At first I think there's no choice but to read one for a second or third time, but then, at the far right end of a shelf, I see a book called *A Canoeist's Sketchbook* by Robert Kimber. On the cover is a nice painting of a canoe on a lake under some blue misty mountains. I pick up the book and proceed to the hot dog station.

"The one closest to you is the only warm one. I just put the others in," says the young clerk.

"OK. I'm taking the one closest to me then."

"That's the only warm one."

I tweezer out the warm red dog and tuck it into the crease of the roll. The roll is soft and doesn't split in two pieces. Ketchup, relish and onions. I don't find any Reese's so pick up a package of M&M Peanuts and pay.

Just when I pull out of the parking lot and read the "200 Cases of Cold Beer" sign for the last time, I take a bite. The hot dog is stone cold, like it's still thawing. I go over the sequence in the store. "The one closest to you is the only warm one." I repeat that in my mind, I know she said it, and I know I picked up the hot dog closest to me. I suck it up and take another bite of cold dog. This could be the worst hot dog experience since fifth grade when I barfed dogs and beans on the cafeteria floor and swore off dogs for forty years. Oh well, maybe the coffee and chocolate will turn things around.

The right turn off the Golden Road—Telos Road—gives notice you're in big country now, and it's getting bigger all the time. From the bridge, there's an iconic view of the Penobscot cascading down toward Big Eddy, and there, framed by forest above the river's tumult, looms Katahdin, cathedral of the North Country. When you cross over the river, it feels like you have crossed the divide. Ahead is the big woods, behind is modern life.

There's more traffic than usual on the Telos Road. Big four-wheel drive pickups, a handful of SUVs, logging trucks, and semis hauling enormous yellow excavators and bulldozers. It takes me a few minutes to appreciate that most of the traffic is for moose season which starts tomorrow. The pickups haul low-slung snowmobile trailers that are easy to drag a moose up onto. Oversized coolers go in filled with beer and come out packed with moose meat. One guy hauls in an old home freezer *sans* compressor for packing out meat. Mountains of tarped-over gear rise out of the pickup beds. Camouflage-covered arms stick out the open windows. An army is mobilizing. Tomorrow morning the troops will take to the woods and start killing moose. By this time tomorrow, scores of animals will be shot dead, gutted, and dragged onto snowmobile trailers. Like all other big mammals in North America, the moose are still here because of game laws. Without them, moose in Maine would be extinct in a few years. The Maine moose population is estimated at 29,000, and in 2010 the Department of Fish and Wildlife issued 3140 permits.

I check in at Telos Gate and continue the northerly slog to Chamberlain Bridge, a major confluence of activity in the North Country. There's a ranger station, maintenance sheds, a put-in for the Allagash trip, a camper parking lot for hunters and ice fishermen. It's a good deal, and if I had a camper I'd park it here too. I stop and stretch and take in the fine views of Katahdin from the bridge. Things are pretty quiet this time of year. It's almost like you have the entire Maine woods to yourself. From Chamberlain I take the Guy Allen Road, pass Miller Time Campsite, a homemade camper condo parking area, and bear right onto the Grande Marche road, the long straightaway up between Umbazooksus and Chamberlain Lake. The route crosses a centuries-old canoe carry connecting the Penobscot and Allagash watersheds, a path less taken now that roadways have replaced waterways as a means of transportation. They've replaced culverts on Grande Marche Road, and the new back-fill is blasted ledge up to twelve inches across.

Finally I make the turn onto the Carry Road, and drive three more miles to the yellow gate. It's 2:30 P.M. I figure an hour and a half to get the canoe and gear lakeside. I wrestle the canoe off the top of the car and onto the cart propped upright on the other side of the gate. Then I put all the gear on the ground beside the canoe. Tent, sleeping bag, sleeping pad, two small dry bags of clothes, bow saw, ax, cooler, wangan, life preserver, small green day pack, a wool jacket, fishing rod, creel, canoe paddle, and pole. After placing everything in the canoe, I pick up one end and start pushing it down the trail, trying to channel positive energy toward my cart which already is showing signs of strain. It's obviously overloaded, but maybe all that creaking is part of the breaking-in period. A hundred feet from the gate (five thousand feet from the lake) the breaking-in period ends when the cart snaps like kindling and collapses to the ground.

One side of the plywood top has torn right off the screws which fasten it to the 2 x 4 of one plywood fork. This would have shown up at home had I done the road test I intended. Fortunately, I anticipated repairs and go back to the car for a screw gun, a baggie of screws, and an antique Kelty pack frame. Everything comes out of the canoe, the cart is refastened, and the canoe repacked, only this time with less gear.

The new plan is to move the canoe a hundred yards, then come back and move the leftover gear up ahead of the canoe. Progress over the Carry is slow. The trail is a cinch for walking, but for a top-heavy, overloaded under-built canoe carrier, it's a rough voyage. The canoe yaws back and forth over the center of gravity, threatening to capsize with every wave. I watch the wheels wobble around and wait for the inevitable.

Five hundred feet from the gate, forty-five hundred feet from the lake, while crossing a rough drainage area, the right wheel meets a rock and kicks hard left. The plywood tops shears off the 2 x 4, and the canoe sinks. The cooler overturns, spilling lamb chops and eggs among the moose droppings. Tea bags, iron frying pan, matches, utensils, and fuel canisters are spread around the rocks.

Now I think I might be in a real pickle. I've hardly started after an hour on the trail. When I pick up the broken top I discover it had been orientated so only three of the plies ran parallel to the wheels. By turning the plywood 90 degrees, I'd get five plies perpendicular to the wheels and increase the shear fifty percent. There's still some hope. I refasten the plywood in the new orientation and load the canoe for the third time.

Now the cart is much stouter and up to the load, but to gain the strength I've traded away stability, because now the cart's wheelbase is four inches narrower. The canoe complains like a princess feeling a pea five mattresses down. I reduce the gear inside by half again. I beseech, cajole, encourage, prompt, curse, and caterwaul. I push, pull, hug, dig in my heels to move the canoe forward and keep it afloat, and at long last attain a final hilltop four hundred feet from the lake. Now the challenge is to keep the canoe from running away downhill. Dragging the stern slows things down, and after a small collision with a tree, we roll out onto the ranger's lawn and down to the lake's edge. Three hours to go one mile, and it's starting to get dark.

Less than an hour later, I have a fire snapping by the edge of the lake, the warm orange flames pale company in the cool dusk. Islands Camp is rocky and rooty and damp, and in my mind I'm already moving on.

For breakfast I fry half a pound of bacon, and then nurse the contents of the coffee pot while loading the canoe, noting this is the fifth time in eighteen hours. I shove off and paddle close along the east side of the lake in the company of some mergansers. The middle of the lake is a cauldron of snarling whitecaps and no place for a canoe. At noon, after four hours of paddling, the canoe scrapes the beach on the east side of Ice Cave Camp. A steep hill shelters the site from the south winds, and there are fine views across the lake and the ridges ripe with fall colors. There are trees close enough to tie off the tarp, a grassy knoll for the tent, a gradual gravel beach for the canoe. I resolve this will be home for the duration of my stay.

The forecast said two or three days of rain starting tonight, so I'm anxious to get firewood under cover. Someone bucked up spruce logs with a chainsaw, which is a nice service because cutting up eight-inch spruce with a small bow saw is close to impossible. After two hours of hauling in wood, sawing it, and splitting it, a respectable pile of dry firewood rises beside the fireplace. Several armloads of dead spruce branches make kindling, and that stuff goes under a small tarp. The new sixteen by twenty-four-foot tarp stretches beautifully over the ridge pole, and provides a drip line four feet out from either side of the table's benches. Let it rain.

By 4:30 P.M. the fire is cracking and companionable in the gathering dusk. Pork chops are on the menu tonight, and reheated roasted potatoes and carrots from our garden. Suppertime in the woods is 5:30 P.M. That leaves daylight for doing dishes and tidying up, and by 7:00 P.M. it's too dusky to read. I take a cup of tea into the tent, snuggle into the bag, and read Kimber by headlamp.

After dark the winds pick up, and the rain starts falling. Rain on the tent is steady and melodic until blustering, errant gusts whip around the point, snapping the tarp and dashing the water out of the trees and onto the tent, staccato and arrhythmical, like a Parker or a Gillespie is out there directing things. The night is wild, and lying on the ground in a tiny tent feels not a little vulnerable in the big dark wet woods. Nothing deters the loons though, and they call back and forth across the black windswept lake reassuring each other. Loons have called over misty waters since the Late Eocene thirty to forty million years ago. My ancestors have walked here less than fifty thousand years. When the wolf crept from the edges of the night into the halo of man's fire, the loon had long called on the waters. It's a great sadness to me that our legacy to the loon has been a poisonous one.

The rain continues all night. I sleep soundly for four hours, but then a wrinkle in the bag wakes me. Then a draft through the zipper. The pillow needs adjusting. My late night imagination kicks in and populates camp with wild animals, floods the tent, fells an old nearby tree, sends me notes from the spirit world. The first people to know loons did not separate the spirit world from their world, the loon world. Then, all worlds were one world.

The heavy rain moves on, but blowsy showers waft around. Tendrils of gale spur the trees as an ashen dawn seeps over the lake. I make coffee and watch the rain drip off the edges of the big tarp. Red and yellow maple leaves stick on top, and from underneath they glow like stained glass. Across the lake the clouds scud low over the land, and vapors smudge the tops of the trees. This end of the lake boils with spumy gray waves.

There is no agenda in camp. At home something always needs attention: a building to repair, a garden to weed, a field to mow, errands, paperwork. At Ice Cave there are few callings. I have to keep an eye on the lake and be mindful of the wind and paddling conditions. There is housekeeping—or camp keeping. Cooking, doing dishes, tending the fire, watching the woodpile get smaller. Visits to the outhouse, keeping clean, brushing teeth. Rehearsing what I'd do if a bear came calling.

By mid-morning the showers have given over to sprinkles—not enough to dampen my clothes or my spirits, so I pack food, jacket, and bottle of water into the canoe and shove off for the inlet and Johnson Stream. A few minutes later, gunshots boom from over the ridge. The big bore booms intended for moose remind me of the caravans of coolers heading north two days ago. I've seen enough gutted moose tied to trailers. I hope the moose got away.

At its mouth, Allagash Stream is somnolent, and alders crown the banks. It makes lazy curves for a mile, then the current steps up. At one bend, a towering pine forest stands on a sandy promontory. One tree has fallen and dammed the stream. I push along a protesting kingfisher, surprise blue herons and mergansers. Moose tracks pock the exposed stream bank. A fine shower bursts on the stream. Over a deep pool, a shred of mist shifts, yaws upward, and evaporates.

Someone has flagged the mouth of Johnson's with a piece of pink tape hanging from a branch. Flagging tape is the alphabet of North Woods language. Garlands of orange notify drivers of a washout. Several strands of blue say turn right now. Right here a couple inches of pink announce Johnson Stream. I turn the canoe into the mouth of the little stream and pry my way through overhanging branches until the canoe grounds out fifty feet in, where the stream turns hard right around an ancient ghost log. The pine log is a forgotten giant, felled long ago with an ax. This pine once stood tall in the forest, sentry to ten thousand winter nights of silent stars and creaking frozen trees, witness to birch bark canoes slipping past. Beyond the ghost log, there's not enough water to float a Popsicle stick, never mind a match, and at last I'm convinced I made the right choice.

I pole back into Allagash Stream, and the current speeds the canoe downhill toward the lake, where big sky opens again, empty and raw, gray and lonely. The loons call plaintive, inaccessible songs, wild and windblown. Back at camp, I make lemon tea and listen to the wind, always the wind. A mile away on the east shore, the wind plays the vast woods like an orchestra. Now a lively trill scuttles through the campsite trees, loosening brilliant red and yellow maple leaves which drop to the lake and bunch up in little painted groups.

Though I have a fishing rod with me and I have wet a couple of the flies purchased in Medway, including the Montreal Whore, my enthusiasm for fishing is lackluster, and I go through the motions with little emotion. Which means I'm not really fishing. It could be I am trying to relive some of my youth, when magic was plentiful, but that has not happened. In fact, I am more relieved than disappointed when I do not catch a fish. But it makes me an outsider, because I know everyone here is a fisherman.

On a paddle up the scenic west side of the lake, I meet a group of three canoes.

"That's a way to do it." one remarks, keeping a close eye on my poling.

"It gives you a lot of power you don't get from a paddle."

"I can see that. How many times you fall in the water?"

"None yet." There are six in three canoes. Camo shirts and hats. Quasi-military-looking canoes. They watch me pole like I'm an alien from space. Poling a canoe is one of the most efficient methods of propulsion, yet many canoeists don't know it exists. Most canoeing is downriver these days, and besides, canoes are not embedded in culture as a survival tool. You don't have to go upriver, so you don't have to pole a canoe. The first thing my parents taught me about boats was you don't stand up in a boat.

"Cut yourself a spruce pole and give it a try. It's not so hard as you might think."

"Maybe. We're headed down to your neighborhood. Good luck."

The lake shore bends west where the big cove stretches back under

Allagash Mountain. The more I turn the corner, the more I meet gusts that head me off. A couple of times the wind grabs the bow and spins the canoe around, and I imagine getting blown across the lake. After an hour of struggle to windward around the cove point, and on a couple occasions getting manhandled by the wind, I turn the canoe around and head back the way I came. The canoe flies over the waves, scudding like a spume of foam.

The three canoes are on the beach at Ice Cave. No one is around, and I assume they are off exploring the caves. I don't see the one asleep until my canoe scrapes the shore and wakes him up. Behind him on the beach is a twelve-pack of Schlitz and a plastic bag of Reese's Peanut Butter Cups.

"How's the wind?" he asks.

"Hard up around the corner. It's coming around both ways. It was behind me a good way down." I take the thirty pound rock out of the bow of the canoe and drop it on the beach.

"We were wondering how you'd make out, being alone like that."

The rest of the guys start turning up on the beach. I see this is a father-son trip, a group where the fathers look young and the sons look old. They check out my canoe with sideways glances—it's a different kettle of fish than their fiberglass canoes. All three are Old Towns equipped with back rests, fishing rod holders, camo packs, and coolers. Let's see. Six guys times six beers a day makes thirty-six beers times, say, five days, that makes a hundred and eighty beers or almost eight cases. That's why Robert Kimber does not recommend beer or wine on a canoe trip. Too much to carry and too many returnables to tote down the river, that is if you're not throwing them overboard. He advocates a good whiskey or some other condensation. Or bring no alcohol. I have none on this trip and I don't miss it, though if I had it I would surely drink it.

After the fishermen leave, I make tea again and walk around the camp listening to the wind on the water and trees. I think about how the human soul formed in the cradle of these sounds. The lapping waves, the seas of tree tops bent to breeze. Therein lies the peace of the world, and therein, too, lies the long fetch of unknown. Animals in the night. Thunder and lightning. The best journeys into wilderness stir the prehistoric soul that slumbers inside us and wakens us to what we share with all life.

The evening steals out of the shadows and spreads across the lake. The damp air blows through camp. I delay my fire because I do not want to go through the wood supply too soon and do not want to fetch more. Tonight I will have baked beans, potatoes, biscuits spread with butter. After today's paddle, it feels like I have done what I wanted to do in coming here, and the chill damp weather is wearing on me. The thought that tonight will be my last night on the lake takes hold. An early start will beat the wind. I build a big fire and begin organizing gear for the morning.

I am up at 5:00 A.M. The sky is cloudy, though one time I look up, and the moon shines like a pale yellow coin through the overcast. I make the coffee wearing a headlamp, my candle in the wilderness. There are protocols to follow. The tedious tent must be folded and rolled with care if it's to fit in its stuff sack. The big tarp will compress to a compact bundle if folded with patience. I push the canoe a little further into the water during loading so it stays afloat. It's a few minutes after 6:00 A.M. and still dark. The wind still sleeps, only a daybreak breath of air stipples the middle of the lake. One shove and the stern of the canoe rasps off the gravel and floats free.

The wind continues to slumber while I paddle up the lake before dawn. There are a few other early risers. Two mergansers, a beaver, and one fish rising next to the canoe. Tendrils of mist curl around the painted flanks of Allagash Mountain. I am reluctant for the trip to end.

At the landing I ground the canoe too soon, well before I can step onto dry land, and when I stand up to pole off, in a moment's inattention my boot snags the rail, and I spin off balance and drop my right foot into six inches of water.

"How many times have you fallen in the water?"

"None yet."

In four trips, everything is at the top of the hill above the ranger station, and from there it's all downhill. I know what to expect this time and start leapfrogging the gear. When everything is at the car, I lift the back hatch, brew coffee, and change into dry clothes. The rain comes and settles in, pours down a steady keening on the forest's fallen leaves.

West Branch of the Penobscot, Two Boys, and I

My son Mariner, his friend Abe, and I are driving north for a few days of canoeing on the West Branch of the Penobscot. The boys are fifteen, going to be sophomores in a month. I'm sixty-one and don't know what I'll be in a month. Mariner's had his driver's permit for a week and has been at the wheel for an hour, sharing the road with the outsize logging trucks of the North Woods. Trucks so large they're illegal to drive anywhere else. I've told him the rules of the road up here are stay out of the way of the logging trucks and look out for moose. He checks the rear view often and is doing a fine job. I can tell the landscape is making an impression.

We're wending our way up the east side of Moosehead Lake on Sias Hill Road, one of the roughest roads around. You used to start this trip at Greenville and paddle the twenty mile length of Moosehead Lake, but now roads provide a shortcut, but perhaps a shortchanged experience. When we reach the Golden Road, Marin turns west. It's only a few miles to Caribou Checkpoint.

Caribou is one of the North Woods gates where you sign in. The gate is always open, but between May and October the station is manned, and you have to pay road use and camping fees. There's a little shack off on the right with an array of solar panels on the roof. Inside, a rat's nest of black wires snarl around a single receptacle in the corner behind the desk. Maine North Woods coffee mugs are for sale on the counter. The agent's mother watches TV from a La-Z-Boy while knitting with pastel yarns something for a grandchild. Great-grandchild maybe. The agent wants to know where we're going. "We're putting in at Lobster, going down the West Branch to Chesuncook." She is writing this information down on my paperwork as I'm speaking. "Then we're coming back up the river to Lobster."

She stops writing and looks over at her mother. "Hmm. So you're not really going down the river."

"We're going down, then we're coming up."

"But you're not really going *down* the river."

"I guess not. If we're putting in and taking out at the same place. Right, we're not really going anywhere."

"Okaaay. Well. Keep this permit with you all the time. The ranger will ask to see it."

A little further along the Golden Road, we see signs for Lobster Dip, a low place among the hills. If you spend much time studying the place names in the Maine woods, you'll see a sense of humor at work. Then a little further again and we turn onto Lobster Trip Road. Up ahead a huge yellow excavator sits on a newly-shaped shoulder. It looks pretty weird out here in the middle of a soft green forest. The machine has been stripping the alders off the sides of the Trip Road, leaving a wide shoulder of slick gray clay. The operator walks down the road with his head tilted at an odd angle, and when we pass he throws a desultory arm in the air.

"Whoa! Did you see the flies around that guy!" shouts one of the boys.

"I saw a gray cloud but I didn't see any flies."

"Oh yeah, they were flies all right."

Holy smokes! That was a lot of flies. One of those tundra hoards you've heard can drive a man crazy. Everyone has stopped talking. All of a sudden I get cold feet. This is going to be one heck of a trip. I wonder if there are any alternatives to being chewed alive in the next few days, but it's too late. We'll just have to make the best of it.

A new steel bridge spans Lobster Stream, and just on the other side is Lobster Landing, a good-sized parking area with a boat ramp and a portable toilet. As soon as we step outside the car, each of us attracts a personal cloud of insects. The buggers are small and light and hover together like a little conversation of mist. I'm not sure what they are— they're not something we have at home. It is incredibly hot, in the 90s and humid as a wet rag. A real long way from the sea breezes that air condition the coast in the summer. Low thunder mumbles in the west.

It takes an hour to get the canoes off the top of the car, unload all our gear, and put it into the canoes. Seems like a lot of stuff, but then it always does. My intention is for the boys to manage their own canoe. Pack it, keep it shipshape, take care of it at the campsites. Abe weaves a rope web over everything. No way is anything getting out of that canoe. We dub it Fort Knots.

We float off the landing, paddle toward the bridge, and wait for a loaded logging truck to cross. A squall of hot dust follows the rig and spreads out over the river. The big steel beams bend, another Lobster Dip. We ease out past the island at the mouth of Lobster and feel the tug of the West Branch current. I reach down and drag a hand in the tea-colored water. Long green grasses undulate dreamily over the bottom. The rank and file of fir and pine close in on the banks. The river is luminous and shines with the bright blue sky. The boys are rapt.

Only a few minutes later, we are in sight of Hannibal's Crossing, the bridge where the Golden Road crosses the West Branch. A couple of logging trucks rumble over it. We're surprised to find a couple dozen young ladies huddled under the bridge abutments. They appear to belong to a summer camp and are waiting for their canoes to be brought down to the river from the road above. My first thought is, *there goes the solitude,* but then, there's plenty to share. Better this group than a swagger of Bud Light-guzzling yahoos, which in fact I have never met in the woods but am always afraid I will. I believe most people who take the trouble to paddle a canoe are going to be reasonable and thoughtful people. Another human in a canoe and I share the same ethnicity. A person on a jet ski belongs to an alien race. When I see one of those things, I want to be armed with an RPG and blow it out of the water. There would be a small oil slick, but at least it would be quiet.

Thunder rumbles closer, and we linger under the bridge for a few minutes waiting for a shower to pass. On the river bottom I see a tire and some twisted steel. A few yards downstream, several bullet-riddled Budweiser cans lie half-buried in the sand.

You can just see Thoreau Island from the bridge. Henry camped on the east end of the island on his 1853 and 1857 trips. It's a thrill to cross these paths in time, not only with Mr. Thoreau, but with all the river drivers, all the Native Americans who traveled these waterways for thousands of years. You can feel all of them because, except for the Budweiser cans, the river hasn't changed much, at least not around here. I want the boys to feel this too, but resist a travelogue lecture. They will take from this what they will, no matter what I say.

We stop at the campsite at the head of the island where I camped for one night in May. Then the grassy knoll was lush and fresh, scrubbed clean by the river's spring runoff. Now, after a summer's use, it shows wear and tear. Tent setups and boot traffic have matted the grass. The ground feels more like a well-used town park than a wilderness island. The boys are unimpressed and itching to keep going. I hold in my disappointment over the condition of the site, but am impressed by their enthusiasm.

We tick off the miles, three an hour without much effort. The next campsite is Smith's Halfway House, six miles down. The squalls continue from the west. Rain seethes over the surface of the river, a reedy, watery sound that winds up and turns down as the showers come and go. An hour later, below a stretch of quick water, we take out at Smith's Halfway House. In the 19th century, Mr. Smith ran a farm here, but there's nothing left of that now, and the woods have long ago taken back those fields. It's a good site on the outside of a big bend in the river. You can see a long way upriver and down, and it's a restful place, the river waters murmuring over the rocks. The boys rig their rods and stand out in the middle of the rainy river casting flies, their lines scribing long yellow loops against the dark forest.

I cut firewood and prepare to start a fire inside the steel fire ring. When I move a large half-burned log to the side, I find some slob has left a cardboard container of chocolate milk, the little blue straw still sticking out of the hole in the top. When I pick it up to put it in a trash bag, the container falls apart, and the curdled chocolate milk sprays over my hand and spills on the ground. I scrape up the stinking curds and wash my hands which now smell of sour milk. While I'm at it, I decide to tidy up other trash minutia left by our predecessors. I pick up several wire ties, a bottle cap, a short piece of rope, and a twelve-inch bungee cord still with the hooks on the ends. There are packaging scraps, a corner of a plastic bag, a piece of a box top.

An hour after we're set up, the girls we met under the bridge arrive in three canoes. *There goes the solitude,* I muse again, but they are a reasonable group. I overhear a man's considerate baritone giving hushed instruction when they disembark from the canoes. A few minutes later, three more canoes come around the bend and come in close to talk with our neighbors. They would have taken out on our site were it empty, but

Ragmuff Campsite is not far below us. One of their canoes almost hits Marin who's standing out in the middle of the river casting.

Between showers we eat our dinner of grilled chicken, peas from the garden, and potato salad made for our trip by Holly. The boys fish again and throw a Nerf football on the riverbank. I retire to my tent soon after cleanup. Can there be a better way to go to sleep? Well fed, tired from the day's travels, the river murmuring over the bones of the earth a stone's throw away, a benevolent sky overhead, now stippled with stars. I have a thin sleeping pad, only a half inch of foam, but I sleep like a stone. I wake up at four. but don't get out of bed until five, when I make a fire, cook bacon and eggs, and toast rolls over the flames. It is a fine morning. We are all itching to get going. The boys break camp and load their canoe efficiently and with some attention to detail.

They start out willi-wagging around on the river. Keeping the canoe going straight is still a challenge. Five minutes downriver, Ragmuff Stream enters on the left. You can hear its waterfall dropping off a ledge some distance above the mouth. The girls are there, and some are awake and moving around the rainbow of tents scattered in the clearing. Over on the right side of the river, a red buoy floats in a back eddy, and I wonder what someone would be marking in the river. I've noticed many of the river rocks streaked with canoe colors, but there are way too many rocks to mark. But wait, that buoy looks like it's moving upriver in the back current. Aha, it's not a red buoy, but a red Nerf ball. Overnight the river had come up and lifted the ball off the riverbank. If they'd missed it, they didn't say anything to me. I pick it up and paddle over to intercept them.

Today their canoe is not quite as organized as when they started out yesterday. They have nearly enough gear to be self-sufficient. Mariner usually travels light—a little too light this time it turns out, as he's forgotten a raincoat. He has a knife and his Jet Boil stove. Abe has his own cook set and utensils, a tube of fire starter paste, and several knives. They have packages of snack bars, water bottles, suntan lotion, and clothes. Two super slingshots rest of top of the luggage. By the end of the paddling day, a lot of stuff will have settled to the bottom of the canoe—shirts, socks, snack wrappers, water bottles, orange peels, and an inch of water. Just like Mariner's room back home, only here he's added water.

Several moose are abroad on the river this morning. A few tolerate our passing them on the opposite side of the river, but others take issue. One or two dripping steps out of the water and they vanish without a sound. We round one bend and see three moose spread out over a quarter mile. The first moose goes into the woods directly, and we put down our paddles and drift toward the next animal which is browsing on the bottom a hundred yards downriver. It takes a moment for the mama moose in the woods to appreciate that the two strange things floating on the water are headed toward her baby who's standing knee deep in the river, nonchalantly pulling her breakfast off the bottom. It's hard to describe the sound a 1500 pound animal makes moving at full speed through a thick forest. That moose is making enough kindling to last me all winter. The boys drift a canoe length ahead, and the racket perks them up.

"Can a moose run across the river?" asks Abe?

"They can run anywhere they want. But not on top of the water."

"Could one catch up to us on the river?"

"I don't think so, if we paddled fast enough."

"I've never heard a moose running through a forest like that."

"Neither have I."

A mile later we come up to Big Island. From the top of its high bluff topped with tall pines, another party of female campers waves to us. If the boys have any thoughts, they keep them to themselves. I go left around Big Island in the smaller channel. It's now forgone that if I choose to go one way, the boys go another. I can tell they like being on their own. I stand up most of the way, but in places I have to get out and walk. I jump three deer which have come down for a drink. A half mile later, the boys are waiting for me in the eddy of a large boulder, and we take a break to consult the map. We are headed for Pine Stream, a flowage that enters the river from the south a couple of miles above Chesuncook and five miles from Big Island. We plan to set up camp early and have time to fish.

Below Big Island, we bang through a mile of shallow rips. A couple of times I get out and walk the canoe. It would help to have better knowledge of the channels which crisscross the width of the river. Lots of the rocks here are colored like canoes: red, silver, green. Then suddenly the river turns sharp right and flows down deep, dark, and swift against sheer ledge. The current boils with whirlpools and upwellings. I tell the boys this looks like a good fishing spot, but they are intent on Pine Stream and don't want to stop. We have, I believe, already passed Fox Hole, a renowned fishing spot where trout hang out in the summer. I had read of Fox Hole in Lucius Hubbard, one of the most poetic and observant of 19th century wilderness trippers, but never did the research to try and locate it on the map.

Not far below the ledges, the current slows and then becomes imperceptible. Early travelers like Hubbard describe running some sharp rips here, but a hundred years ago, Ripogenus Dam raised the lake and drowned several miles of the West Branch. Where Pine Stream feeds in the river looks more like a skinny lake. On the north side, a wide low meadow opens the landscape to a big great plains type of sky.

Half a mile out from Pine Stream, I encounter five otters. Their heads are so far out of the water that it looks like they're standing on something. They stare at me intently, barking and hissing like I'd better get a move on out of their neighborhood. There are five heads, and they move in concert—they dive together and surface together as if they were connected. If you didn't know better, you might take them for a five-headed lake monster and name her Chessie. With her quintuplet head, hissing complaints, and bristling whiskers, Chessie is intimidating. I'm not too disappointed when she drifts away upriver toward the boys. When I land at the campsite, a moose strolls across the meadow on the other side, continues into the river, and starts to swim over to my side.

We no sooner set up camp than the boys have their fly rods out and are casting from the ledges. I watch their personalities telegraph through the arcing rods. Mariner's rod arcs forward and back in long even strokes, and the line drifts above in sinuous slow curves. By contrast, Abe's delivery is fast action. He whips the rod back and forth like he's trying to see how fast he can go.

"Abe, slow it down," says Mariner.

"I can't," says Abe.

The most annoying feature about Pine Stream turns out to be red squirrels. I've had personal space invaded by these critters before, but these guys take the cake—and the bread, the crackers, the trail mix, the pancakes, and any edible thing left untended for more than five seconds. They are unafraid and don't care they're not wanted. At last, a practical use for the wrist rockets. I don't try to hit them, but a fusillade of half a dozen rocks sends the squirrels back to the underbrush for several minutes at a time. They scratch around in the leaves, pretending they're making a respectable living on nuts and seeds.

Toward evening fish start rising on the river, and the magical little circles excite the boys. They rig up again and prepare to take out a canoe. All afternoon the western sky has brooded with a sullen dark brow. By the time they're ready to go, big raindrops are coming out of the sky.

"Don't go far." I say, already settling down in my tent. There's no easy chair out here, and the best way to take the weight off weary bones is to lie down on my sleeping bag inside the tent. Especially when it's starting to rain. My tent is new and has hardly had a chance to show its mettle. It feels a tad small for a tent claiming to be a two-person accommodation, but tonight I'm more interested in the tent's waterproofing than its spaciousness. For three hundred bucks, I'd better stay dry.

The boys have just started out on the river when lightning flicks through camp. Low thunder follows, then anxious laughing and canoe paddles slapping water. I look out the little porthole in the side of the tent and see them paddling madly in reverse. Another flash and I hear them counting the seconds until the thunder comes. They take cover in their tent which they perched within splashing distance of the river. It's an all-out squall now. Maybe it's to dispel some vulnerability they feel about their location that they shout out the seconds between the lightning and the thunder.

It's an all-night rain and a heavy one, but in the morning the tent is dry, and I decide I like the tent despite its odd shape. The boys are sleeping in a borrowed tent, and they wake to find the bottoms of their bags in a small pond. To be fair to the tent, the pond likely had something to do with the impermeable stone they pitched it on.

"What else is wet?"

"Not much. A few little things."

After years of use, the fire pit location is sunken, and this morning a deep moat surrounds the fire ring. Last night the boys burned all the wood I'd stored under the tarp, when they could have picked up dry wood anywhere. So there's no dry wood, and no one's inclined to take up the challenge of making a fire in the sodden conditions. I make coffee on the stove under the tarp. Everything under the tarp is wet too, but at least now the rain falls straight down, and we have shelter to eat cereal and bread and butter. This gives the boys an idea, and after breakfast they set to building a cover for their canoe.

They collect some sticks and rope and a tarp and start assembling. I can imagine the outcome but don't say anything, while a light rain, not unpleasant, continues through packing and construction. It takes an hour and a half of tinkering before they are ready to go. I've had lots of time to check camp for stray items, and on a last look over the far side of the ledge, I find the red Nerf ball floating in a puddle.

For half an hour the boys struggle inside their tarped-over canoe. Abe can't see where he's going and follows Mariner's directions from the bow. They geegaw back and forth more than usual. A family coming downriver comments on the rain and gives their canoe curious glances. After a mile of paddling, I overhear talk inside the tarp about getting to shore and "taking this thing down."

"Dad, we're stopping."

"OK." (Good idea).

An hour later we are paddling against the river current. We stop at the ledges for something to eat, and the boys rig their rods. Abe is out first, and within five minutes has caught and released five chub. The dark swirling waters look promising for brook trout. You can catch a chub any old time, but the brook trout are elusive this time of year. Marin and I come up empty, and I feel a little bit of fishing envy going on. Abe hooks one deep enough that the fish dies coming off the hook. He cleans the fish and puts it in the cooler to eat later.

The chub, though a member of the minnow family, can grow to fourteen or sixteen inches. We only see them around eight. Many fishermen consider them a nuisance, and I can see why if you're interested in brook trout. But for the boys, chub are better than nothing. Their nests are works of art. The males build the nests by picking up stones in their mouth and making a pile on the bottom of the river. They use stones very equal in size, about an inch, inch and a quarter in diameter, and they start with a base two feet across at the bottom and add stones until they have a cone with a single stone at the top. The piles are symmetrical and sculptural—beautiful to look at through the tea-colored water. In one quarter-mile stretch, we see dozens of nests—some several feet deep below the surface, and in this time of low water, sticking up in the air. The rock pile is not a nest in the conventional sense—it works by the female depositing her eggs over the top of the rocks, and then the males come by and drop their sperm. The young fish use the interior spaces between the rocks for shelter.

Now the toughest part of the river lies ahead, a mile or so of Class I current. I pole most of the way. The boys try poling but it does not go well, and I overhear comments as to the wisdom of a canoe trip that goes upriver. At one stretch we have to get out and drag the canoes through shallow rips. The rain comes down so hard the surface of the river boils. Water is everywhere. The air hisses with falling water. It's a good thing it's warm.

Our destination for tonight is Big Island. The boys amuse themselves through the drudgery of upstream work by calculating time/distance equations to estimate our arrival time. How far 'til the island, how many paddle strokes per minute, how many per mile, how fast over the bottom, percent of their paddling capacity they're exerting, how many strokes at eighty percent capacity, a hundred percent capacity? How long could they paddle at a hundred percent? When will we get there? They run through a set of calculations, discover an error or change a parameter, then start over. Whatever conclusions are arrived at, we do reach the upriver end of Big Island, the island with the high bluff where the girls waved to us yesterday. The rain squalls have cleared out. We lug our gear up thirty feet of log steps and drape wet gear and clothes on the bank to dry.

After so much rain, fire is reluctant. Several attempts later, I give in to Abe's suggestions to use his fire starter paste. I've never seen this stuff and am curious. It's like grease coming out of a toothpaste tube. A match set to a blob under a fistful of spruce tinder and birch parchment brings a fire to life, though with everything so wet, it burns like it's got a governor on it.

We cook a batch of rice, mix it with some soup, and sit down up against a big pine log at the edge of the bluff. There is a fine view up the river. Once again the rising fish excite the boys, and in no time they're back out there casting from the canoe. After cleaning up and sorting wet stuff on the river bank, I settle into my tent and write. My sleeping pad, though adequate on grass, proves thin on roots, but even that doesn't stop me from falling asleep with a pen in my hand. When I wake up hours later, the tent is black as a coal mine.

The night is calm, and in the distance I hear sloshing footsteps moving downriver. Closer and closer comes the sound, and I've no doubt it's a moose out for a late night stroll and something to eat. It seems to take an hour for the animal to work his way down past the island. It's not the first time I've wondered how well moose can see tents in the dark. Later, awake again, still in the blackest of nights, I get up to go outside for a whizz. The sky is brilliant with pointillist yellow light, and the spangled scarf of the Milky Way streams overhead across the starry dome. The river whispers its watery asides. Standing at the brow of the bank, I see yesterday's rains have swelled the river, and the water is rising under the boys' canoe which is not tied. When Mariner took his boots off, they were four feet above the water level, and now they're at the water's edge. I creep down the steps and make adjustments.

At 5:00 A.M. I sit down with coffee and watch the early morning mists coil over the water and swirl downstream between the island and Ouellette, another campsite directly across the river on the mainland. In contrast to the pine wooded island, Ouellette is a grassy and open site that looks unused. A hare hops into view and nibbles on the grasses without paying much attention to anything else. A minute later a bald eagle lands in a tree fifty feet upriver. Then a moose materializes out of the river vapors a hundred yards upstream and moseys toward me along the bank opposite Ouellette, stopping now and again to put his head under water. The hare is aware of nothing. The moose may be aware of the eagle but doesn't care. The eagle is aware of the moose and me. I am aware of four beings when I notice a v-shape moving upriver. The new arrival is a beaver. After a few minutes the beaver, the eagle, and the hare are gone, leaving only the moose and me. When he puts his head under, I get up and pour more coffee. He meanders around for a hour before he steps onto the bank, takes another step, then disappears into the forest. It's time for us to move on with our day too.

During cleanup Abe wipes his rice bowl from last night. Several gobs of rice get away from him and fall on the table. He takes a swipe, and the rice sprays across the ground. The white kernels on the dark ground look like maggots.

"Whoa. What if everyone did that? They'd be garbage all over the place. Then how would you like to be the next person to stay here?

You've got to pick it up."

Abe gets it right away, and with good humor gets down and cleans up the rice, now all mixed up with pine cones and pine needles. Mariner and I kneel down to help.

After the kitchen is put away, the boys turn to packing up their bedroom while I tidy up around the site. We've dragged a lot of wood into camp and dropped it off to one side. It's a mess of brushy spruce branches and odd-length logs. After a few minutes breaking up kindling, sawing the logs to length, and stacking them, I notice the boys are watching me sideways while folding their tent and rolling up sleeping bags. I can tell what they're thinking. *We're leaving and he's sawing firewood?*

"Remember," I say, "it's leave no trace. Think of yourselves as guests here. The idea is leave it for others as you'd like to find it yourself. There was a firewood supply when we got here, and there will be firewood when we leave."

"Umhmm."

It seems to take forever to get everything loaded into the canoes. Up and down the steps a dozen times, carrying down the gear we carried up eighteen hours before. A last look around once, a last look around twice, a last look around a third time, and we shove off. No sign of the Nerf ball this time. I start off poling, and the boys paddle. Soon they are a quarter mile behind, then further. We have ten miles to go. The original plan had been to spend another night on the river, but we're so close to the car, it's starting to feel like the last day on the river. The boys feel the same—that thing about a trip being over in your mind before it's physically over. We decide to reach the car, drive to Millinocket for dinner, and go home. We need to be back early in the morning anyway, and there's no good place to camp close to the car. We settle in for a slog upstream. Only the quick water by Smith's will pose an obstacle, and as it turns out, the rain has raised the river enough so it's not a problem.

I pull over at Ragmuff Campsite to use the outhouse. Ragmuff Stream, swelled by the rain, spills a corona of foam into the West Branch When we were coming downriver, you could pass by Ragmuff and not notice it; now the current spilling into the West Branch pushes my canoe around.

Ragmuff looks a little ragged, the uncut trampled grass unkempt. I am feeling grateful for the convenience of its outhouse, though when I open the door I am almost asphyxiated by the sickly odor of air freshener. A spray can sits on the platform. The natural odors issuing from an outhouse are nothing you want to breathe deeply, but the synergistic chemical stew of outhouse nature and the can contents are disgusting. The ingredients on the can read like a who's who of carcinogens. The intrusion of American prudery into my canoe trip really annoys me. Who would trade the smell of shit for cancer?

By the time I'm back at the canoe, the boys have caught up and we open some grain bars and drink water.

"How's the poling going?"

"We only have one pole, so we're not poling."

"Why do you only have one pole?"

"We forgot one at Big Island." Since they were not so keen on poling anyway, I think I understand. I don't want to sound like a jerk, but there are some things to be learned here.

"Just remember these paddles are not poles. No pushing off rocks with paddles. Now, if you look at my paddle I haven't even scratched the varnish."

"Umhmm."

After Ragmuff the canoes stay closer together. Depending on the current I move ahead, then they move ahead. Abe says he remembers all the bends in the river and predicts how many more turns before Thoreau Island, where we plan to eat lunch. They know Thoreau Island is only a couple miles downstream from the car, a goal they are anticipating with growing fervor.

"From here," says Mariner, "there's one turn, two, three, then that straightaway, four, then you're at the island. I'd say two miles until Thoreau Island."

I don't say anything about the distance. I know we've at least six miles of paddling. "We have a perfect day on the river," I reply, "don't be in a hurry to get off."

The eagle we follow up the river takes their mind off the uphill paddling. Sometimes we see it far in advance, other times we're almost on top of it before it lifts off and flies further ahead. It's hard to tell. Maybe we're seeing more than one eagle. A couple of times the bird takes off and leaves downy white feathers floating in the sky, which drift lazily down to the river. In one encounter we see the eagle sitting on a branch over the river. We pull over to the opposite bank to give the bird as much space as possible, but he flies off anyway. This time a primary flight feather comes loose and somersaults once, twice, before the heavy quill end points down, and the flight path follows a vertical chord down, the quill end leading the big brown spinning blade, describing perfect helices before landing on the water. We had all three stopped paddling to watch the flight of the feather.

"Let's go get that feather," says Abe.

My first thought too, but I make no move. I like the idea of the feather floating downstream without being disturbed.

"You're not supposed to have eagle feathers," says Mariner.

"But I want an eagle feather," said Abe.

"There's a ten thousand dollar fine for possessing an eagle feather."

"Why is that?"

"Because, they're endangered, and they won't know how you got the feather."

"Hmm."

Most of the river along this stretch is between two and four feet deep, making it perfect for poling, and standing in the canoe allows a fine view of the bottom. In the backwaters and eddies, thousands of pulp logs left over from the river drives lie on the bottom in pick-up-stick profusion. The last drive on the West Branch was in 1971, so the youngest logs have been in the river forty years. During spring freshet, the currents lifts some of the logs up onto the banks, and when the melt water recedes, the logs dry out and regain their lost buoyancy. Then a big rain like last night refloats some of them, and a vestige of the old river drive comes alive. We pass a couple of the ghost logs drifting sluggishly downstream.

Freshwater mussel shells lying open on the bottom shine with a pearly iridescence. Small alluvial plains of gravel form fan shapes behind larger rocks. The current is relentless. Around each bend we expect to see the island, but over and over there's another straightaway of river ahead. After six hours of poling, my back aches to beat the band. Abe and Mariner banter alongside me.

"I see the island," says Abe.

"That's not the island."

"Then it's around the next bend."

"You said it was two miles away two hours ago, Abe."

"I miscalculated."

But at last there is the last turn, and we float into Lobster Stream, where we find the current has reversed itself and is now flowing upstream into the lake. Lobster Stream can flow either way, depending on the weather, because Lobster Lake and the West Branch are so close in elevation that when rains swell the West Branch, it pushes up into Lobster Lake. It makes no difference to us what direction it flows. The canoes scrape the beach. The trip is over.

Mariner drives out to the Golden Road, turns toward Millinocket. He glances often at the rear-view mirror, keeping an eye out for logging trucks. We are headed to Pelletier's Restaurant in Millinocket for an early supper. It's a new restaurant with a truck on the roof, and inside there's a huge tile mural of Pelletier men posed around a loaded logging truck with Katahdin in the background. These guys have starred on TV's *American Logger*, and now have their name on a new restaurant. I think dinner there will make a nice closure to the trip.

"Well," I say, "that was a good trip. Did you guys have a good time?"

"Umhmm."

"Umhmm."

Mariner only drives a few miles to Caribou Checkpoint, then says he's tired.

"Why don't you want to drive anymore?"

"I'm too tired."

A few minutes later the Apple iPod 4 is on.

"What are you doing on that thing?"

"Driving."

Outside our windows, the North Woods landscape slips by, and they have their noses in media. I try to ignore it. Half an hour later nothing has changed except the level of my impatience.

"Now what are you doing?" I ask Mariner, whose thumbs are twitching.

This time he smiles. "Fishing."

Our canoe trip really is over. We're back in the real world of video games.

Katahdin—a Solo Climb

The door of the car at the lean-to next to mine opens, click! Then closes, chunk! A minute later again, click, chunk! My address is Lean-to #11, Katahdin Stream Campground, Baxter State Park. There are four lean-tos strung out here, hunched under tall pine and hemlock and jammed between the stream and the Appalachian Trail which is close enough behind me that I could spit across it. On the open side of the lean-to there is a picnic table and a fire ring in an area of bare, packed ground. Sitting at the picnic table, you can see the clear mountain water gargling over the rocks of the stream bed. Only a dollop of sun ever reaches the stream as it tumbles down from the heights of Katahdin. It's so cold it runs gelatinous, a molten flowage of wrinkles. It's so clear it has a fantastical quality—like it's too good to be true.

Click! I wait for what's coming. One and, two and, three ...chunk!

The tumbling stream is loud—it runs too fast and frenetic to be soothing—but it's not loud enough to drown out my neighbor's car doors opening and closing. Vehicle access to these sites is a major attraction and a major drawback at the same time. You drive right up to your campsite and don't have to carry anything far. Or not at all. Need something? Get it out of the car.

Click! it goes again. Chunk!

I've come up here alone at the end of September to climb Katahdin. I'm sixty years old and have never climbed the mountain alone. My last climb was humbling. A year ago, as a chaperone with my son's eighth grade class, I climbed the mountain with five adults and twenty teenagers. For most of my life I would have been in the lead of such a group, but this time keeping up was a struggle. I've shed ten pounds since then, but I'm also a year older. I am looking forward to climbing on my own terms, and I suppose some of why I'm here is to find out what those terms are.

So far as I know, I can still do the things I've always done, only more slowly. What I've learned about aging is it's like joining a conservation program. You want to save what you have and use it the smartest way you can.

Katahdin Stream Campground is a base camp for climbing Katahdin. It's like Roaring Brook Campground and Abol Campground in that way—almost everyone is here to climb the mountain, but at KSC there's also Appalachian Trail traffic. All AT thru-hikers and section-hikers come through here. There's a lot of coming and going. In season you need a reservation to park your car for the day, and a park ranger directs traffic until the lot fills. Some people come and spend a night, get up early to climb, come down, and drive home.

There's a big range of experience among hikers. Some day trippers show up to climb in street clothes, looking like they're out for a day of mall shopping. Then you've got people with the thru-hiker patina, and they stand apart as you'd well expect them to after hiking two thousand miles. Long hair, beards, browned skin, lean bodies, bulging backpacks, and serious hiking gear are some of the signs. If you were blindfolded, you could detect an upwind thru-hiker.

I consider some of the differences between them and me. They carry all they need on their backs. For this three day solo trip, I have filled the back of my car. My cooler alone exceeds the capacity of one of their backpacks. In my cooler are the same things you have at home in the refrigerator—eggs, bacon, butter, cheese, milk, cold cuts. I like cold orange juice in the morning, and a chilled bottle of vitamin water after a day on the mountain. I also have two sleeping pads, a real pillow, and a big bulky cotton camp-style sleeping bag, the most comfortable thing there is for sleeping outside. My sleeping bag alone would fill a backpack. Throw in a bag of clothes, camera, binoculars, twelve gallons of water, an ax, a camp stove and bottles of fuel, hiking boots, sandals, a piece of rope, first aid kit, day pack, and the flotsam and jetsam of hiking paraphernalia—compass, knife, maps, pens, writing pad, dark glasses, handkerchief, walking stick, hat, windbreaker, water bottles, plastic bags, toilet paper, matches, and whistle. The thing is that I know in advance I won't use most of this stuff, but I don't have the will to wean myself from the security it provides, so I make the choice to waste time finding it, organizing it, packing it, unpacking it, looking for it, trying to remember if I brought it in the first place—then taking it all home and repeating all the steps in reverse. I take a deep breath and sit inside the lean-to with my back against the logs and listen to the stream. From here I can't see any neighbors. The irony in coming to Baxter is that I have far more contact with people here than at home, where we don't see any neighbors, only fields and trees. We see way more turkeys than people.

My next door neighbor is a gentleman from Maryland who is preparing his dinner. His car doors are like kitchen cabinets. When I cook something, I find all the ingredients and set them on the counter before I start. That way everything is within reach during preparation. This gentleman retrieves one thing a time. First the passenger door opens and closes. Then the rear door, then the passenger door, then the rear door again. Click chunk! Click chunk!

The park stained the outside of my lean-to brown. They left the inside unfinished, but the surfaces are not untouched. They are covered by an alphanumeric mosaic of initials, dates, and messages left by ancestral campers who have mistaken the walls and ceiling for a guest book. I amuse myself looking for the oldest signature. It's carved into a log in block letters about three inches high: J. Doyon—July 5, 1937

All the early signers used a knife—they really carved their initials back in the old days. Nowadays pilgrims use a marker. KDS used a pink marker on 7/25/09. I can't find any obscene messages, though the writing itself is obscene in a way. It seems to be accepted here— it's too late to do anything about it anyway—but up at South Branch, signs posted in the new shelters ask campers please not to write on the buildings.

Click chunk!

My neighbor is driving me nuts. With only a little forethought, all his opening and closing car doors would be unnecessary. I practice my camping etiquette lecture. "Campers should be seen and not heard."

Click chunk!

I expand the lecture. "If you took your stuff out of the car and put it on your table, it would be within reach, and you would not have to open and close you vehicle doors every thirty seconds. You would save a lot of steps. Your door latches would last longer and you would not be polluting the campground with your car noises." After rehearsing my talk several times, I feel guilty and unfriendly. After all, we likely have things in common. We could be the same age. He's alone. Maybe he's terminally ill, and this will be his last visit to the park. Maybe it's his only visit. Maybe he's here alone because his wife died last month. He's probably climbing Katahdin tomorrow, and maybe he's a little nervous about it.

By 8:00 P.M. I'm snuggled down inside my camp bag and am merging with the stream. The car doors have gone to bed. It's hard to imagine getting much sleep, between the watery ruckus and the moonlight—bright enough to read by—filling the lean-to. I wake up several times, and the stream assures me the earth's hydrological cycle is unbroken. The moon seems to hang around forever. In the middle of the night, I think it's strange so many people unknown to each other sleep soundly in proximity—in open shelters with all their gear and their bodies spread around with no security.

I sleep in 'til six, an unusual event. Blame it on the cozy cotton camp bag and surplus of fresh air. I make a pot of coffee and eat a bowl of grainy cereal and an orange. Lean-to #11 is the last stop for coffee, so I drink the whole potful and plan for a second breakfast on the trail after my appetite has kicked in.

Into my day pack go four liter bottles of water, three hard boiled eggs, sunflower seeds, raisins, apricots, sliced turkey, sliced cheese, chunks of steak left over from dinner, an apple, and several buttered white rolls. Gear includes a windbreaker, a cap, a long-sleeved wick away shirt, windbreaker pants, camera, binoculars, map and compass, handkerchief, and a watch.

The sun is still well below the mountains in the east when I start the hike. It's a good day. There will be many on the trails today. Every trailhead in Baxter Park has sign-in sheets, and I check in on the Hunt Trail at 6:45 A.M. Three hikers signed in twenty minutes before me, but I doubt I will see them. Most people on the trail will pass me, not the other way around, and I wonder how long I'll be on the trail before I do see someone.

For the first mile, Hunt Trail ascends beside Katahdin Stream which now trills and gushes up from the depths of its scoured bed, and now runs a muffled gurgle away through the trees. Though the grade is easy, you have to pay attention where your feet fall, because the trail terrain is roots and rocks. Taking your eyes off the trail is like texting while driving.

A mile in I reach Katahdin Stream Falls, a popular destination for day hikers. The falls are dramatic. The curling ropes of white foam splurge down the green moss-clad ledges. Above the falls the trail changes from gradual to steep. Decades of erosion have ditched the trail two to three feet below the natural grade of the mountain, but that's about to change. I find a makeshift mason's shop set up under a tarp. Trail crews are building new stone steps that will transform the sluice into a stairway. Comealongs strung through the trees haul rocks up from the stream bed a couple of hundred feet below. It's a comforting sight and a sign that we are taking care of the mountain.

After another hour and a half of steep climbing, the trail emerges from the confines of the woods into wide open daylight and a notorious section of the trail called the Boulders. Upon seeing the boulders, many climbers decide they've had enough and turn back, and I can see their point. It's a rumble-tumble mess of rocks that look like an avalanche put on pause, and not a place to be if you're uncomfortable around heights. One question in this climber's mind is *when is the avalanche going to start up again?* I know we're talking geologic time frames here, but even the geology clock has to tick sometime.

When you're among the boulders, your usual terms of reference are turned upside down. There's lots of air on the one hand, implausible gulfs of space, then a sheer wall of rock. Maybe it's the unpredictable juxtaposition of rock and air that now and then prompts one to drop down onto all fours. Even so, all goes well until I meet head-on two imposing stones ten feet tall. This obstacle would be like stepping over a grain of sand to a free climber, but for someone with a preference for the ground, the rocks are intimidating. Fortunately, someone solved this dilemma long ago by installing a couple of wrought iron bars at a strategic location. They are much like handicap accessible grab bars, and with these handholds and some shimmying and shaking, I grovel over the top, sprawled full length on the ground. Once atop this little nubble, I don't think about it or look back, but move onto the next rock, then the next.

Once you get started, the thing is to put your head down and go. That's what the trees up here do to survive. They keep their heads down. In fact the forest looks like it's shrunk. Though the species up here are the same ones that will grow one hundred and fifty feet tall a couple of thousand feet below, at this altitude they are called krummholz, wind-stunted vegetation the elements mold into a dwarf forest three or four feet tall. No doubt if one lived up here, he would acquire a physique gnarled and thickened like the trees. I can feel the krummholz in my bones when I stand up to the wind.

The Boulder passage does not last long—maybe twenty minutes, but more than enough time for your heart to start bleating for a stretch of level ground. And then, as if on cue, out of the blue—or into it—your next step draws you out onto a wide swath of flat white gravel that looks like it came out of a Japanese landscape book. This reprieve continues for fifty yards, and on the south side of the trail there is space to sit and get out of the wind. I take out a hard boiled egg, some peanuts, apricots, and a bottle of water, and take in the views.

Looking out across the land from four thousand feet above sea level, your eye sees no evidence of human endeavor. Maybe that's part of the attraction mountains have for us. Somewhere in the collective brain, a memory of the earth as Eden survives. But since then, layer upon layer of culture has dulled a primal perception of earth and cut us off from nature. Not only does a climb like this transcend our personal travails, but communion with the mountain can connect us to our primitive brain. These heights of Katahdin will strip you raw and bend you low as the krummholz. The mist of a cloud drifts across the sun and make me shiver. Down below I would not give the cold a second thought. Up on the mountain, the cloud's shadow portends.

From the beach, you look up the trail at the craggy rocks disappearing into the blue heaven. The rocks are much smaller than the boulders, and handholds abound. I simply put one plodding foot in front of the other until, in the blink of an eye, I am through the Gateway, the terminus of the hard climb, onto Katahdin's plateau or Tablelands—five hundred acres of treeless tundra—rocks, grasses, lichens, and plants that belong to an ecosystem that elsewhere exists five hundred miles north.

The trail is wide and open. It even goes downhill for a while, a white meandering track set back from the rim and heading toward Thoreau Spring, a mile away. I feel like I'm bouncing off the ground with the weight of the steep climb off my back.

On top of a mountain where there is no potable water, a landmark named Thoreau Spring raises your expectations. In my experience, the word spring connotes a bubbling source of clear potable water, and even though the literature cautions against that image, I'm still disappointed. The Spring, at least this time of year, is more a patch of damp mud, but further on I do find a stagnant black puddle. One legend has it that Henry stopped here on one of his ascents, but none of Thoreau's writings mention the spring, and from his own writing it sounds like bad weather forced him to turn back before he even reached the Tablelands.

The spot is pleasant, though, and invites reprieve from the climb. Other trails intersect here. A hundred yards south, Abol Trail drops off the plateau and follows an old slide straight down the mountain. Cross Trail heads north and cuts across the Tablelands to the Saddle Trail without going up to Baxter Peak, the true summit of Katahdin, still a mile and a half distant. From the spring I can see the rocky vestment of the Knife Edge bearing off to the right of Baxter Peak which, by some distortion of perspective, looks higher than Baxter Peak, although it is not.

From the spring you can see most of the mile of trail arcing up the side of Baxter Peak, and spread out along its length, small groups pick their way over the rocks. Parties converge and separate quickly. Two groups going away or toward each other walk a combined four miles per hour—that's a mile covered in fifteen minutes. I pass several pairs of young climbers around college age, and half a dozen older guys like me, I guess in their sixties. Men outnumber women five to one. One gentleman stops to chat and tells me they are staying at Kidney Pond, and that "she's there now, reading."

Baxter Peak is a hubbub of coming and going, exclamations, people jockeying for photographic advantage. A pilgrim who has ascended via the Saddle Trail bursts onto the peak.

"My God, you call that a trail? No one responds. "At home we would have some handholds installed on a slope like that. Phew! Do you mind?" he asks, extending his camera toward me. "Over by the sign. It's only me. She hurt her back a few years ago. When she saw the trail she decided to stay back."

It's not a day for lingering on the summit. Besides, the descent fully occupies my thoughts—I'm more nervous about going down than coming up, and after a few minutes I'm retracing steps toward Thoreau Springs. At the last moment, I decide to return by Abol Trail. Mother Nature planned this route in 1812 when a section of the mountain succumbed to gravity and slid from a high steep place to a lower flatter location. Today it is still a wide avulsion on the mountainside, visible for miles, devoid of any vegetation, and looking like it happened last week. *Why here?* you ask, and halfway down there are some clues. Right in the middle of the slide smooth domes of bedrock protrude through the loose overburden of gravel and stone. Material lying on top of this bedrock and reposing at such an angle would have a tenuous grip at best. Frost, heavy rains, a lightning strike might have loosened the adhesion, and things just started rolling. They call it a slide, but it's really an avalanche. Down, down, down I go, straining against the pull of gravity which wouldn't give a hoot if I slipped on the ball-bearing gravel and fell a good long way. Just to make a point, a football-sized stone lets loose and clatters down the slope.

This flank of the mountain faces due south, and the sun's rays hit it square on. What a contrast to the bone chilling environment on the summit. It's hot, my feet hurt, my back hurts, and I have a low grade headache, probably from dehydration. The slide seems to go on forever. Every few minutes I check the back trail for people behind me, but thankfully no one shows. I like to keep the footballs in front of me, not behind. By the time I get to the trees, my water is gone. After several false alarms, I hear the sounds of Abol Falls percolating up the mountain through the trees, and then a little further on, unmistakably, click! chunk! and I know I'm back.

A hiker driving a Subaru rescues me from the dusty Park Loop Road, and makes short work of the mileage between Abol and Katahdin Stream. Back home I am elated to see #10 empty, the gravel all raked out for the next guest. But it's short-lived elation when I come around the corner and find a white station wagon parked at #12, and several people milling around talking loudly. I open a bottle of vitamin water and listen to an argument about tent placement. They set to getting everything out of the car, one item at a time, opening and closing the doors each time. One guy whistles while he sets up. I think about dusting off my quiet campsite lecture, but instead head out for a swim. I have to drive a few miles up Nesowadnehunk Valley to reach the stream, but it's worth it. The chilly plunge is short, but changes everything. The frigid mountain water is like a transfusion, and the hot trail dust washes away.

Back at #11, clean clothes make me feel new. I get the fire going, pour a glass of wine, and lean back on the pillows propped against the wall of the lean-to. There's lots of activity along Lean-to Alley. Over in #12, they are preparing for tomorrow's climb and getting ready for bed at the same time. One of the women crawls into the back seat of the car to change into pajamas. After dark a small car with a leaky muffler pulls into #10. It's a hard right turn into #10, and the car's headlights sweep back and forth, back and forth through the foliage before the driver gets it right. Two women talking in low, earnest voices unpack and set up in the dark. They make no fire, and their campsite is soon quiet.

In the morning, the women get up before me and drive away in the dark. The loose muffler on their little car pants at the early morning effort. Likely they are headed to Roaring Brook parking lot from which they will climb Katahdin by Chimney Pond and the Saddle Trail. My neighbors in #12 are awake and moving too. They pack up and relocate their car to the day parking lot. I pass one of the guys coming back from the outhouse. He wears a red bandana on his forehead and his hiking poles click on the road. There's a bounce in his step. His friends are waiting for him.

"Wow!" he says with a broad smile.

Katahdin—We Can Do It

Holly and I have been talking about climbing Katahdin all year. Longer than that. We've been talking about it for several years. We missed a chance in the spring, then before we knew it we were in the thick of blueberry harvest, and during blueberry harvest we don't think much about climbing mountains for fun. And then, just like that, summer's over, the boy is back in school, the hours of daylight are on the wane, and so are the chances for getting up to Baxter before winter. The weather for the weekend looks good, and we decide to toss our hats in with the thirty thousand other pilgrims who climb Katahdin each year.

A check on Baxter's online reservation system shows all the campgrounds at the Katahdin trailheads are full, but there are openings at Nesowadnehunk, one of my favorite places in the park, and we make reservations for two nights at Lean-to #2 at the north end of Neso Field. I have not stayed at Neso since they reconfigured the lean-tos, so am not familiar with the location of #2. However, the lady at Park Headquarters says, "You can see Doubletop Mountain and Squaw Bosom, or whatever they call it now," from the site, and that's good enough for me. Now all we have to do is pack.

Because I instigated the trip and am not working full time, provisioning and packing falls to me. This can be a trying but satisfying task, and it better be, because by the time you've collected gear from attics and cellars and garages and closets, shopped for food and packaged it, you've probably put as much time into preparations as the trip itself will take—at least that's the way it seems to work around here. Insofar as a journey is in large measure a state of mind, you are well on your way by the time you start packing and buying groceries. This metaphysical stage of the trip should be experienced with pure satisfaction because you are not going to experience flat tires, forgotten wallet, biting bugs, sickness away from home, travel delays, or terrorist plots.

Between trips I imagine a system whereby all our camping equipment is stored in one location, clean, packed, ready to go. Lead-in time would be short and efficient. But the reality is when the next trip comes, nothing's changed, and the required items have been dispersed and infiltrated into every domestic venue and must be sought out, sorted, assessed, and packed. This time, because we are driving to our campsite, there are few limitations to what we can bring.

The camp kitchen is pretty obvious—everything needed to cook over a fire or a stove. You might think these items would be found in the kitchen, but everyday kitchen utensils are not allowed to leave the house for the woods. Instead we rely on second-string items relegated to the basement or attic. The centerpiece of my metaphysical kitchen is the wangan, a custom built pine box where everything "kitchen" lives during the trip. Pots, pans, utensils, cups, bowls, plates, salt and pepper, matches—all in one place ready to go when you are. But we do not have a wangan yet; it's out there on the cosmic to-do list, and this time I will pack kitchen things into a wooden apple crate, a milk crate, and a plastic dish basin.

I track down a frying pan in the basement, forks, knives, and spoons in the attic, a saucepan in the garage, back to the basement for the camp stove. I tell myself it's good training for the mountain. Sleeping bags and pads are over the garage and still lying loose and rumpled from being dropped there after a visit by out-of-state cousins. The day packs shoved into a corner after the last trip need cleaning out, and inside is a bonanza cache of wilderness stuff. A headlamp, the right knife, the compass, the first aid kit, a roll of toilet paper, a notebook and pens, toothbrush and paste, a windbreaker, a hat, a water bottle, a box of strike-anywhere matches in a baggie. I collect all this stuff onto a big table so I can see what's there and hopefully, what's not.

Notes on items

Kitchen:

The centerpiece of the camp kitchen is Holly's mom's #11 Griswold, an eleven-inch diameter cast iron frying pan with "Erie PA" stamped on the bottom. Griswolds are the Cadillacs of cast iron frying pans, and the inside of this one is so smooth and shiny you can see your reflection in it. However, the inclusion of old #11 into the camp kit is not by unanimous vote. I'm for it, but Holly is only half for it, which means the yeas have it, more or less. However since the pan came down on her side of the family, her vote weighs more, so it's a toss up. I make a lame statement about how her mom would be pleased her pan supported her daughter's first ascent of Katahdin, and the pan squeaks by onto the "go" list. A two-quart cast iron dutch oven rounds out the iron inventory. Where #11 has a mirror finish, the Dutch's interior looks like rusty 80-grit sandpaper, and no objections are raised at its inclusion. It's been hanging on a nail in the basement for twenty years, after all. These two items alone equal half the weight of a backpacker's entire outfit, but such are the luxuries of car camping. Nor are there any reservations concerning a spatula and fork from a long defunct barbecue, the moose antler handle knife I made, a combo salt and pepper shaker, or the two burner Coleman stove and propane canisters.

Food:

I always start with good intentions and a list, but at the store old habits take over, and I buy what I want, no matter what the list says. Two people camping out of a car for a few days do not present a challenge in terms of volume or weight, and there is no need to employ the scientific method for planning camp meals. Our cooler is the size of a small refrigerator. We can pretty much buy food like we're buying it for home.

We do try to pack for zero waste, which puts some limits on choices. That means no bananas unless you're planning on eating the peel. No apples unless you eat the core. No store packaged chicken unless you eat the plastic wrap and foam tray. Instead, we buy dried raisins and apricots. We repack meat, cheese, cereal, energy bars into zip lock plastic bags we can wash out and use over again. I have never achieved zero waste however. Something always sneaks in—a baggie tie, a bottle cap, the inner seal of an orange juice container.

Clothes:

These are easy to deal with in the summer. We like things to be in order when we take off, though, so we do all the laundry we can find, even if it's not going on the trip. A change of t-shirt, several pairs of socks—you can't have too many clean socks—underwear, and jeans for after the climb, a windbreaker, sweatshirt, and towel. Sounds simple, but it's hard to believe it takes most of a day to get this outfit for two ready to pack into the car. Lists are checked, rechecked, rewritten, checked again. Holly has her own lists, and we must compare. What about the binoculars? Are you bringing long underwear? Do you think we'll need bug dope? No, certainly not, the bugs are gone.

Before packing, I pull the Pathfinder up to the garage and clean out the pitcher's mound dust, loose straw, fast food wrappers, and the odd peanut M&M. It takes an hour to pack the car, fill the coffee cups, and let go of home. If we don't have it now, we're not going to need it. Check the stove, unplug the toaster. Whatever.

It's a three-hour drive to Togue Gate, where a park ranger comes out to talk and check our paperwork. Nesowadnehunk is another seventeen miles up the Neso valley, and driving at the Park's 20 mph speed limit, that's another hour of driving along a one-lane winding road. It starts out following an esker, and through the foliage we get glimpses of Katahdin, views that stir the imagination and quicken the blood. The road climbs steadily up the valley beside the Nesowadnehunk River. We pass the white cross marking the grave of the Unknown River Driver, a point of interest that's seems of suspicious origin. A few miles beyond the grave, the wet gray cliffs of Doubletop rise up sheer and shadowy across the river, and then at Ledge Falls the river drops in silken sinews over smooth granite bedrock. The pools between the drops are prime swimming spots if you can take the bone-chilling mountain water. Then a couple more miles of sharp curves where all the trees have their back skinned off and we emerge into the big sky and old farm fields of Nesowadnehunk Campground.

We have a little map of the campground we printed off at home and use it to find Lean-tos #1 and #2 which are set apart from the other single lean-tos, recently relocated to the old Group Field. At first glance, it looks like these sites offer more privacy than the lean-tos in the Group Field, and for visual privacy that's true, but their proximity to two group sites make them vulnerable to sound pollution.

These are walk-in sites. That means you park just off the Tote Road and carry your stuff to your lean-to. It turns out not to be too long a lug, and after five trips we've transferred everything from car to camp. Lean-to #1 is empty for the time being, and we hope it stays that way, because the path to #2 passes within forty feet of #1, the open front of which is oriented toward the path. Not an arrangement that allows much privacy. Nor does the site of the outhouse located beside the parking area, which means that every time a tenant at #1 needs to go, he or she must walk through the front yard of #2. Sometimes the site planning at the park leaves me scratching my head.

The park looks to have been on an outhouse-building boom for the past couple of years, and they've done too good a job locating them where visitors can find them. Outhouses are everywhere, and are often the first thing you see at places of interest. The good side of this is you're never far from relief. The downside is the prominence of outhouses in the park landscape, as if people come to the park specifically to stop and use them. It does seem they could have sited them more discreetly without compromising function. Not only do outhouses impact the views, they also emit odors which at this time of year are often powerful. When we parked in Lean-to #2's lot, the fumes whacked us as soon as we stepped out of the car. Locating the outhouses a few feet into the woods would have made a big difference.

After we move into our modest eight-foot by ten-foot log walled structure, we make a pot of coffee and sit down for a breather to enjoy the views of Doubletop. From the north, Doubletop could be called Singletop because the two peaks line up, and only the north one is visible. The flanks of the mountain rise out of the valley in elegant symmetry, and the result is a perfect paradigm of a mountain, so well-formed and picturesque. Doubletop from Neso is one of the finest views in the park. We have not been sitting long before a breath of air wafts the smell of urine into camp. *How could that be with the outhouse so far away?* I wonder, but the answer is obvious in a moment. Only five feet from the lean-to, a path worn in the grass disappears into some accommodating bushes. The outhouse is two hundred feet away. It doesn't take a Hercule Poirot to solve this one. Over the dry, hot weeks of summer, our predecessors at #2, probably the males, have opted for the convenience of the bushes instead of the long haul to the outhouse.

From Site #2 it's a short walk to the ranger's cabin located on the east side of the bridge over the Neso River. A visit to the ranger station's porch hastens your immersion into park life, which, for all its amenities and bureaucracy offers plenty of sustenance for the soul. There's a clipboard hanging on a nail, a pencil on a string, and instructions for signing in. There's a separate pad for leaving the ranger a note. There's a log book where visitors are encouraged to record wildlife sightings or any other observations of note.

Posters stating park rules are stapled to the wall. The rules are simple. Don't feed or try to ride the animals. Pick up your trash and take it with you. Carry in, carry out. Be quiet after 10:00 P.M. Don't make a fire where you're not supposed to. There's another poster about what to do if caught out in a lightening storm. It's got a photograph of several young people with their hair standing on end, and some fine print saying everyone in the picture died. There are instructions on how treat hypothermia and dehydration, and pointers on what to do when you meet a bear or a moose. There are warnings about how the weather on the high peaks can change for the worse in short order. Advice on what to do if you get lost. How much water to carry. The symptoms of heat stroke. There is a notice about not bringing in firewood which may be infested with the wooly adelgid and or the longhorn beetle, and a notice about not carrying rock snot from one waterway to another via a boat or trailer. All these directions seem pretty manageable. To my mind, these notices illustrate the attraction of living in the park for a few days. There are no notices of taxes, no doctor's appointments or political campaigns, no home invasions or insurgent activity or car crashes. In Baxter all you have to do is follow a few simple rules, and you are living well. There's no question you are on a short umbilical cord connected to the wider world, but that's OK. I'd rather meet a bear than a politician any time.

Across the road from the ranger station is a woodshed stocked with bundles of firewood. Three dollars for twelve pieces of split firewood tied up with green baling twine. They leave a loop in the twine so you can pick up the bundle and carry it a short distance before it starts cutting off the circulation in your fingers. I did bring a bow saw and ax, but there is not much firewood in a field, and the woods close by are young without standing dead wood. This is a vacation, so we can afford a few bundles of firewood without feeling guilty, can't we? We rummage through our pockets, find enough cash for four bundles, and deposit it into the cash box on the shed.

Evening spreads still and quiet through the Neso valley. Tomorrow's Katahdin climb overhangs the campsite like a teetering boulder. Holly adjusts her day pack while I tend a steak and a veggie burger. "What time are we going to leave? How much water shall we take?" Potatoes, carrots, and onions from our garden sizzle in the Griswold. A diffuse but annoying plague of no-see-ums ride in on the slanting rays of warm afternoon sun and make themselves a thorough nuisance. Before you know they're even there, they've come and gone, leaving behind an intense burning itch that lasts half an hour.

"Did you bring any bug dope?"

"No, there weren't going to be any bugs, remember?"

When the food is ready I reach for the plates, but there are no plates. There is no way not to admit I forgot plates. However, we can eat right out of the pan, I say with pleasure, and place old #11 in the middle of the table with a knife and fork on each side.

At 7:30 P.M. we duck out of the no-see-um feeding frenzy, bury into sleeping bags, and wait for the itching and the voices we overhear from Group Site 2 to subside. Darkness comes down around the ring of mountain peaks, shadows deepen along the alder edges of the field, the blue opacity of the heavens slowly turns translucent, and a complexity of stars begin to glow in the heavens. The orange fire burns with bright companionship. Smoke from fires all across the Neso Valley unfurls straight up, then hits a temperature inversion and drifts lazily downriver toward the east. Then comes a long sound sleep. I wake at 4:00 A.M. to a hushed pale of waning moon bathing the field. Dark Doubletop reposes in the south. Above the mountain, Orion lies on his side in the lonesome aura of predawn sky. The only movements are the ghostly smudges of shape-shifting fog riding the shadows of the sinking night.

I've been watching the leading edge of a dark gray cloud slide our way from the west. After the coffee perks, and before Holly is out of her sleeping bag, some ice cold white objects fall out of the sky and splat on the picnic table. Couldn't be. I drag the picnic table in under the lean-to overhang as far as it can go and sit down. Couldn't be snow. In no time the table is soaked, and the weather convinces Holly there's no hurry getting out of her sleeping bag. Precious minutes tick by. We've a big mountain to climb. Are we going to let a few raindrops affect the day? Yes, but not for long. Just like that, a swatch of blue cracks the gray and all is not lost. The girl weans herself from the warm cocoon of the bag, and we get on with breakfast. Oatmeal with raisins, grapes, fried toast, orange juice, and several cups of coffee.

"That oatmeal seemed watery."

"Maybe that wasn't instant oatmeal."

"I think you were supposed to cook it."

"I think you're right."

You need to make a reservation to climb Katahdin this time of year. If you're not camping at Roaring Brook, Abol, or Katahdin Stream, the three campgrounds from which the major trails for the mountain start, and if you're not willing to hike the extra miles from outlying campgrounds to Katahdin trailheads, you need a parking space in one of the three lots, and this time of year, the lots fill up and close early in the morning. Three days ago I reserved one of three spaces remaining for Saturday, August 28 at the Katahdin Stream day lot. I printed out the pass at home for presentation at the gate upon arrival. They instruct you to leave the pass on your dash for the duration. It's a minute past 7:00 A.M. when we turn off the Tote Road into Katahdin Stream.

A lady park ranger directs traffic coming into the Katahdin Stream lot.

"Climbing the mountain?"

"Yes."

"Park right over there next to that car, close."

"OK."

Several other cars pull in after us. All around people are pulling gear out of vehicles, taking off a layer or putting one on, hoisting packs onto their backs, pulling hiking poles out full length and testing them in the gravel. Click click! Click click! Traffic is heavy at the local outhouse. Both of us use it. There's one more outhouse opportunity after leaving the campground. Katahdin Falls is a mile in, and so popular a destination the park built an outhouse there. After that you're on your own. We adjust straps, shimmy and shrug to get the load right, and then we're off. Five miles to the top.

In the weeks leading up to this event, we have experienced some apprehension—some self doubts about climbing this mountain. We've had foot problems and shoe problems and questions about stamina and physical fitness. It doesn't matter what I say, doubts hang around us like a cloud of no-see-ums. I try offering some inspiration. "It doesn't matter what you feel at the start, because after ten hours of hiking, everything is going to hurt anyway. Any discomfort you feel now is nothing compared to what's coming, so don't worry."

We pass a couple of thru-hiker types chatting in the clearing. Within the park, this trail is called the Hunt Trail. To the wider world, it's the AT Trail, or Appalachian Trail, and this section is the last few miles of a 2175 mile sojourn that starts in Georgia. Thru-hikers are hikers who do the entire trail at once. Section-hikers work on completing parts of the trail over time, maybe years. "Thru-hiker" is reserved for the select group that does it in one season. The thru-hikers we see today are all male. As a group they appear tall, fit, and not in a hurry. They have a demeanor that sets them apart from weekend pilgrims like us. They have nurtured a spareness of body and mind and outfit in order to make the task at hand manageable. You're not going to find any cast iron Griswolds in any of their packs. And no bacon and eggs cooked over the fire either. I do admit a trace of envy when I see these folks. It's not so much they've hiked the distance, but more they've figured out how to do something our society does not expect you to do. In some way they've said, *I'm not doing that* (usually what's expected of you), *so I can do this* (the thing they're not expecting you to do). Three cheers for the thru-hikers and section-hikers of the Appalachian Trail.

We sign in on the Hunt Trail Log at 7:13 A.M.. We're thirteen minutes behind schedule, about the duration of the dawn snow shower. Five or six parties have signed in before us, a dozen or so people, the first energetic souls at 5:20 A.M., almost two hours ago.

There's plenty of time to wake up along the first mile, a gentle ascent beside Katahdin Stream to Katahdin Stream Falls. By the time we reach the falls, two couples half our age have passed us. Watching them from behind is like seeing your own youth across an impossible gulf, and as they disappear around a corner, you feel the pulse of time and the irretrievable quality of youth. We keep putting one foot in front of the other. There's nothing else you can do.

Katahdin Falls, last outhouse call. They weren't able to dig much of a hole here, or they didn't bother, because the pile of shit inside the outhouse is higher than ground level outside. I wonder how they clean this site, and can't think of anything other than shoveling the shit into containers and hiking the stuff out. Maybe there's another way, but no matter what that might be, from here on the bathroom is woods and rocks. The park publishes a *Wildnotes* newsletter, and in it are toilet protocols for the backcountry. You have your below-tree-line procedures and your above-tree-line procedures.

For number one below tree line, get two hundred feet off the trail and go on a rock if available instead of vegetation, so animals won't make a mess trying to get at human salts. For number two, dig a small hole and after use, cover with excavated soil and humus, then leaves and twigs. Carry out used t.p. in a plastic bag.

Above tree line, get off the trail and pee and poop on gravel with no digging, so as not to disturb rare plants. Same rule about carrying out paper. Pretty simple, though I wonder why the park is not urging pilgrims above tree line to carry out their own waste. We do it for dogs on city streets and town parks. Why would a human not carry out his or her own waste from an environment like Katahdin? Because it's yucky, that's why. Apparently we have not caught up to the dogs yet. We'll see how the pilgrims are doing from here on up.

We encounter the first errant toilet paper a mile above the falls. Within arm's length of the trail, a huge flat rock tilts against another in such a way to make a tunnel cave. You could walk right through the structure if you wanted, but you don't want to because at one end there's a deposit of toilet paper. Probably someone who didn't have to go back at the falls or someone who did but didn't take the time. Too bad. My usual inclination to pick up trash is sublimated, and we walk on without entering the cave. We are, we think, not far from the Boulders, a stretch of trail noted for its rugged and challenging terrain. Along the way we pass several locations strong with the smell of urine. A short spur of a path off the main trail, a trampled opening in the brush beside a large rock. These are locations that by their macro geography provide an opportunity to drop trousers and let fly. They are hardly two hundred feet from the trail, and really, who's going to go two hundred feet off the trail in this landscape? Fear of getting lost or falling probably kicks in at twenty feet. Besides, no one's watching.

The trail leading to the Boulders is quite steep. In several locations, huge rocks clog the trail, so you have to find an handhold like a rock or tree and drag yourself up over the top on your stomach. After we've negotiated two or three of these, Holly comments this is a "rugged trail." I don't say anything. In a few more minutes we meet the Boulders. You can tell you're there because the trees all of a sudden are shrunk, and you're looking straight up at boulders the size of small houses. Things are getting interesting.

The original Katahdin was formed during the Acadian Orogeny in the Middle Paleozoic about 350 million years ago, when an erratic piece of continent floating around on earth's crust bumped into another land mass, and where they met the Appalachian Mountains formed. But everyone knows the glaciers of only ten thousand years ago are the master sculptors, and what a legacy they left here. Boulders spilled helter-skelter, a behemoth balanced on a diminutive, rocks eroded to something that looks alive. People get to this point and turn around. Indeed, we meet a young man heading down, crawling on his hands and knees. At first I think he must be injured, but then I recognize the body language of fear. An older man coaches him. "Now pick up your left hand and move it over here. OK, good. Now pick up your right hand..."

There's no question this can be intimidating country. From the loopy flight path of the trail, the mountain falls away thousands of feet on the right and the left. If you're not looking straight down at your feet, you're looking straight into a long-distance gulf of air. What you feel here is more a fear of outer space than of heights. Sky is down, nothing's level, it's tough to find a place to stand more than a couple feet square. People keep moving. You don't see much stopping and taking it all in. It's more like, *let me out of here.* "Don't get too far ahead of me," Holly says. "I'm not usually scared of heights, but I've reached my limit here."

There are exceptions. I am on hands and knees groping over a granite dome when two boots skip by headed down. The boots are laced to the feet of a satyr already fifty feet away, skipping, hopping, flying over crag and chasm. The upper part of the wiry creature wears a scruffy beard and a wool shirt, the bottom half is a fine specimen of mountain goat, sure-footed and spry. *Tra la, tra* la, he sings, *tra la.* It's half man, half goat. No fear of outer space for that man-goat.

Between the Boulders and the final ascent, there's a pleasant respite on the trail I call the beach. Here's a place to take a few consecutive level steps on a settled stomach. There's enough room to sit down and have a bite to eat while taking in the heights of your accomplishment thus far. We chew mixed nuts, cheese, cereal bars, crackers, apricots, and chase it all down with lots of water. The beach also offers private places to pee, not two hundred feet away apparently, for now and then we detect familiar odors wafting through the rocks. You can't really fault anyone. To pee is human. Not everyone on the route is a professional climber with the skills to get two hundred feet off the trail. Better an odor than a broken ankle at four thousand feet.

From the beach on up, the climb looks more intimidating than ever. But now there's no choice. Everyone knows it's harder going down, and no one wants to see the boulders again, at least not so soon, so the only way is up. The trail is increasingly steep, but the rocks are small and offer plenty of handholds. It seems wherever you reach for a handhold, there's one worn into the edge of a rock. It's like this section of the trail was made with humans in mind, and that's a good thing for us, because now the wind picks up and starts to push us around. The sky blackens, and chilly vapors rush up from the valleys below.

"This wind is really strong. I don't want to get blown off the mountain."

"It's strong, but most of the time it's blowing you against the mountain, not off it."

"Oh. Really." I believe Mr. Thoreau on one of his climbs might have felt some intimidation at Katahdin's primeval weather. He made his own trail, somewhere over to the east, at first following a stream, then walking over boulders and Krummholz, a primeval landscape that prompted his observation that mountaintops are among "the unfinished portions of the earth."

And then in the wink of an eye, you step out of it, like you've gotten off an escalator, and emerge onto the Tablelands, a treeless plateau of lichen-covered boulders and grassy plains inhabited by many species of rare plants which do not otherwise occur in these latitudes. There's still an hour to reach Baxter Peak, but now it really is a piece of cake, and for a while the euphoria of mastering the trail carries you along almost without effort. Bit by bit though, I start to feel a new reality in my legs. I try to ignore the aches, but gradually the betrayal deepens and I have to admit I am tired. The last half mile to Baxter Peak, the trail trends upward again, and we have to push it. We see people standing around on top. Lots of people.

Pilgrims start to pass us going the other way. There's a big spread in profiles. There are well heeled, professional-class-looking hikers tricked out in knickers, expensive hiking boots, state-of-the-art wick-away jerseys and jackets. These folks are often smiling, confident, and happy to be where they are. On the other hand are the cotton sweat panted and sweat shirted pilgrims traipsing along in street sneakers. Some of these folks look like they'd been watching TV with a barrel of popcorn when someone got the bright idea they should go climb Katahdin. A lot look like they'd be happier if they'd stayed on the couch. But that's the beauty of this mountain. For all its raw majesty, Katahdin is the people's mountain.

The top of Baxter is 5268 feet above sea level, a painful twelve feet short of a mile. Early pilgrims made up for this deficit by constructing a thirteen-foot-tall cairn at the top. Only problem was some pilgrims felt entitled to take the mile-highest rock home with them, so the mountain shrank back. Then it would get built up again, then it would shrink back. Today the cairn's about eight feet tall. People hug it and get their picture taken with a pile of rocks.

We sit down near a group of college-age guys. They are eating prepared meals out of brown aluminum envelopes.

"You got the chicken and noodle...my favorite. Did you heat it up?"

"Yes."

"I like to heat it up, then put the rest of the heat in my back pocket."

Whatever.

One of them has an electronic device out—I'm not sure what these things are called anymore—propped on a rock so he can watch the screen while he eats. He picks it up and puts it down, picks it up and puts it down. One time he picks it up and brings it close to his face.

"Hey, I've got four bars."

Behind us a bare-chested fellow celebrating his summit lets out a curdling "Yeehaa."

We're a few feet from the beginning of the Knife Edge, a true description of a rock pile heading east to South Peak and Chimney Peak a mile away. A family with several small children eats lunch and takes pictures while discussing the hike. Two of the smaller kids and one of the adults sit backed up to the sheer precipice of the Chimney. They jostle each other getting ready for a picture and smile for the camera. It's too much to watch.

People wait in line to have their pictures taken with the Katahdin summit sign. A lady starts a loud speech. "This man is a thru-hiker and he wrote a book about it."

"Any thru-hikers here?" asks the white bearded thru-hiker.

"He did, he wrote a book about it."

The group of college kids has lapsed into an intellectual conversation. "Yeah, the biggest part of learning a foreign language is learning how to fake it."

"Ha, ha, ha."

There are probably a hundred pilgrims up here. A few birds. I see a junco. Some kind of sparrow. Someone has dropped an apple core on the ground and not picked it up. On the other side of the crowd, a group breaks out with "Happy Birthday." I suppose with all these people, it had to be somebody's birthday. This is kind of like a big party where nobody knows anybody. The guest list changes all the time. Climbers arrive from below at the same time others decide the party's over. I wonder what time the last lingerers will start down and Baxter Peak will once more be only wind and rock. You could climb up here at night. With the moon it would be easy. You could get up here in the middle of the night and wait for the sunrise, and there wouldn't be anyone singing "Happy Birthday" or screaming "YeeHaa."

Going down is not so bad. You can see where you're going, for one thing. At one point among the boulders, I encounter the strong smell of poop. I must be mistaken, I think, because there are no outhouses for miles. Then, not far below, standing on a postage stamp of level ground, is a family of four I recognized from the summit, but right now they are a family of three looking a little sheepish. Somewhere off to the side, family member four has his butt hanging over a cliff and is doing number two.

Halfway down the mountain, the strategic sections behind us, we anticipate camp, and our conversation turns to calculations.

"How much further?"

"Well it's a mile and eight-tenths from the cave to the falls."

"Which one was the cave?"

"That big overhanging rock?"

"No, where the paper was."

"How far?"

"So half mile at least to the falls."

"I think I hear the falls."

"Or is that the wind?"

"Now I really hear it."

"My knees are hurting."

"Mine too."

"I'd like to check out of this trail right now." Meaning the clipboard.

"Now how much more?"

"One more mile from the falls. That's a flat mile."

"It's still a mile."

We are bone-tired at the bottom. Leg, knee, hip, and shoulders screaming.

"I did it, she says, smiling broadly.

"Yeah, you did, and I'm proud of you. "A kiss. Two kisses. A drink of water. One more visit to the outhouse in the parking lot. Big sighs as we settle into the car's upholstered seats. We stop for a freezing swim in the river at Ledge Falls, then back home to start a fire, heat up leftovers in old #11, and drink a glass of wine. Neighbors have moved in next door, and they come over and tell us there are two moose in the field by the road. We take a look at Momma and baby moose, and then we're in the sack. No excuse needed tonight.

At 4:00 A.M. I stir and start writhing out of the sleeping bag.

"Are you going to the outhouse?" asks Holly.

"Yes."

"Watch out for the moose. I almost walked into it. It's sleeping on the path and it growled at me."

"OK." I start out on the path toward the outhouse two hundred feet away. You feel vulnerable walking outside half-naked looking for moose in the middle of the night. Moose shadows are everywhere, and before long I decide to turn back. I find a handy spot off in the bushes not far from the lean-to and take a whizz there. Fall is coming. Rain will come too. Lots of rain, I hope.

Nesowadnehunk and Howe Brook

My address is Lean-to #6, Nesowadnehunk Campground, Baxter State Park. It's mid-week in late August. They told me at Togue Pond Gate I'd be the only one here, and so far that's true.

"Not even a ranger. He's been off for a few days," says the ranger at Togue Pond.

"That's the way I like it," I reply.

"I don't blame you," she says.

But here I am in one of my favorite places in the park and not all that happy. I'm alone, it's hot, and bugs are flying around my head being a nuisance. After all the anticipation, it never occurred to me I'd feel homesick when I arrived. I miss Holly, the cat, and Mariner. He's only had his driver's license a week, and a vague feeling I should be standing by just in case erodes my peace of mind. I sit disconsolately on the edge of the lean-to and wonder if I should have stayed home and worked off items on the fall to do list.

After a few minutes of moping, I get out the park maps and consider what I might do. I already know I'm not climbing Katahdin but can't decide what, if anything, I do want to climb. I had imagined sitting back and reading, and maybe working on some of the pieces in this book, but already the landscape's magic has gotten into my blood, and the urge to get out there in the middle of things has taken over. Mountains OJI, Coe, and North and South Brothers are respectable peaks a few miles down the valley along the Tote Road, and Doubletop's northern trail head starts right here at Neso. I like that idea because I don't have to get in the car to go hiking.

I am alone at the campground, but there are intrusions. Planes drone several thousand feet overhead. Cars headed to other destinations rumble over the gravel Tote Road. Late in the afternoon, a red SUV turns in, rolls down the field, and stops with the engine running. They've noticed the view of the mountains down the valley, and a man jumps out of the car with his camera. He disappears down one of the lean-to paths. The fact they've taken the liberty to drive through the camp field when they're not staying here bugs me, but all I can do is wait for them to leave. The man comes back to the car after a couple of minutes and holds up a finger that says *one more minute*, and he's off again. A minute later he's back again and says into the car window, "There's a bunny down there and he didn't move." Mom and two kids get out of the back seat and all four go to look at the bunny that's not moving. The driver remains in the car with the motor running. I wonder how they're all related, the two men, one woman and two kids. Two minutes later they're all back at the car. "It's a blind bunny," says the woman to the driver. "The bunny can't see, it's blind, and it didn't move."

Red wine precedes dinner which is steak over the fire and green beans from the garden. After cleaning up I read and doze in the lean-to while showers patter on the roof. The four foot overhang is comforting in the rain, and I try to estimate the breeze it would take to push the water in as far as the raised floor where my bed is. I fall asleep early, but for some reason the night is a long one of turning over and pillow adjusting, and long times lying awake watching the stars and clouds.

At last daylight oozes through the clouds. What gives? Today is supposed to be sunny, but maybe it's something to do with the mountain air, and it will burn off. I start cooking on a too-hot fire and burn the bacon, then compensate by under cooking the eggs. They're so runny I put them back in the pan. I used to cook a good egg, but lately results have been going downhill, and I wonder if there's some age-related reason, some realm of perception vital to egg cooking that's slipping away. However, in the next few minutes, the toast over the fire is done to perfection and puts that issue to rest, and I turn to packing supplies for the day. Jar of peanut butter, bag of mixed nuts, and a bag of dried cranberries. A blueberry bar that will not taste good. Three water bottles. Then the hiking requisites: camera, knife, compass, windbreaker, map, matches, cap, and dark glasses. I know darn well I will not use a knife, a compass, or matches on a day hike. These items you carry for the unexpected, and to avoid the embarrassment of having left camp without the essential things if you do get lost.

From Nesowadnehunk, Doubletop is a soft bulbous pyramid, like a well done child's rendering of what a mountain looks like. It's handsome from all directions in the way it rises out of the blue valley and holds itself so solidly in the sky. Once on the trail you see nothing of the mountain, though. One of the ironies of mountain climbing here is being immersed in the leafy woods. Remnants of Hurricane Irene passed over the park a week ago and dumped almost ten inches of rain and the woods are still wet. The humidity under the canopy must be a hundred percent. At the same time it's cool, and that makes my skin clammy and uncomfortable.

After three hours of climbing, I emerge on a small granite outcropping where a few krummholz fir poke their heads above cracks in the rock. A few clouds, head high, scud across the sun, their shadows falling miles away across the valley on the flanks of Katahdin. Almost straight down the Nesowadnehunk River, a cream-streaked coffee-colored vein, flows toward its meeting with the West Branch of the Penobscot several miles away. Aside from a small bridge over the Nesowadnehunk and a distant ribbon of road winding toward Millinocket, no other signs of mankind intrude in the vast landscape. For ten minutes the mountaintop is mine, and a blissful place it is, the sun soft and warming, the water in my water bottle cool and refreshing. I take out the map, align it with Katahdin, and sort out other mountains between us. Then, too soon, voices carry from the South Peak Trail. A party has climbed from the south side of the mountain, has reached the "other top," and is moving toward me. The voices come and go, but in a few minutes, two hikers pop out of the trees and onto North Peak. They're soon followed by another pair, and another and another and another, until ten people have clambered by. The boys in the group mutter a "hello" and some manage an erstwhile glance, while the women smile and offer friendly greetings. They're a good group, but their presence chases away the sublimity of the mountaintop, and I start to think about moving on. After eating nuts and cheese and trying not to drink too much water, I start back. I pass the group not far away, and it's the same reception. The girls look up and smile, say "how's it going" and "have a good day," and the guys look at the ground and wait for me to be gone.

Back down through the rain forest. I amuse myself formulating Hiking Theory #1: all hikes are longer than you want them to be. It never fails—I want to be at the top before I am. Going down is worse, my knees are scolding me and admonishing there will be joint replacements to pay for this abuse. Once more the air is cool and clammy and uncomfortable, and I stop several times to rest and drink. The final mile of trail traverses the north flank of Squaw's Bosom. A moose has passed by not long ago, but I see no wildlife in person, though a woodpecker drums away somewhere up Bosom. Then, near the end, the gentle gargle of the Nesowadnehunk River lifts through the forest and soothes my tired brain.

The round trip is just six hours, which is what the hikers' in-out times on the trail register indicated. A couple of solo hikers did it in five and a half, and some of the larger groups took seven to eight hours. A good hike, and nowhere near as bone-numbing as Katahdin which is four miles and four hours longer. With rest stops, lingering over views, and the obstacle course nature of woodland hiking, I figure about a mile an hour for distance over ground.

Back at the campground, some new arrivals have set up a tent directly across the field from #6. The rest of the campground is empty, and they set up there. At first I try to be circumspect, and that works until the couple drives in and starts talking. That's when I walk out to find the ranger who is back from vacation and making his rounds. He okays my move to another site—for a $15.00 site change fee (something new in park regulations)—but can't confirm the new site is available for two consecutive nights because the gate has closed. I decide to risk it. I back the Pathfinder up to Site #6, open the gate, and throw the whole kit into the back. Drive a quarter mile around the corner, and park at #2, a walk-in site where everything has to be carried two hundred feet. Whole move accomplished in 45 minutes—campfire burning, wine poured, notebook open, wonderful view of Doubletop across the old farm field. Before bed I stoke up the fire and converse with the flames as the dark draws down the valley.

In the night rustling foliage wakes me. From the sound, it can only be a moose or a bear. I don't want an animal snuffling around the camp, so I yell out a "Hey!" from inside the lean-to, and the animal lights out down the edge of the field, accompanying himself with a kind of truncated agitated oinking. I'm sure it's a bear. The ranger had warned me about the bears coming into the field for blueberries. I scouted the field for shedders, and did see a lot of trampled vegetation. "Put your food in your car" he said. I think of the food in the cooler beside the lean-to, and how I'd considered pissing on the cooler before bed. Human urine is an excellent deterrent to wildlife, and pissing on the cooler is much easier than hauling it up into a tree or carrying it out to the car. It's also a practice company might object to. The animal must be far away by now. I can't hear it, and the sound of the river sleeping in its own bed returns to my bedside. After the bear, sleep is reluctant, and I am feeling bad for yelling at him.

The morning of my second day starts slowly, even though I'm splitting cedar kindling at 5:30 A.M.. The morning fire is essential, even though at three dollars a bundle, it's easy to see dollar bills burning instead of firewood. You can collect firewood from the woods, but this is a vacation, and I decide to splurge on a few extra bundles of wood. Besides, Neso isn't the best place to gather firewood, and I didn't bring a saw. The buckwheat ployes soaking in homemade maple syrup are a little on the heavy side, but they're always on the heavy side, and they should stay put for a while. I take time cleaning up and drinking coffee. One stroll around the camp turns up an artifact someone tossed into the bushes. It's a chewing tobacco tin—Grizzly brand. "Long Cut Wintergreen," it says, "Moist Snuff. Net Wt 1.2 oz." There's a grizzly bear image on the top too, and then on the bottom one third of the label, the words, "WARNING: This product can cause mouth cancer." On the back of the can is another warning. "WARNING: This product can cause gum disease and tooth loss." Thanks for the warning, but why stop with Grizzly wintergreen? How about a warning for our chemical saturated culture? Caution: Living in the United States may cause cancer. Caution: Breathing US air may cause cancer. Caution: Eating US food may cause cancer. Caution: Living in this building may cause cancer. Caution: Wearing these clothes may cause cancer. Caution, caution, caution.

OK, the coffee's gone and it's time for a plan. I decide to drive to South Branch Pond to check out the campsites there and maybe take out a canoe. I doubt there's much cause for cancer in those plans, at least in the short term. One bottle of water, a bag of nuts, and what's left of the cheese, fare that will wear thin before the end of the day, though the jar of peanut butter is buried in the pack and will stave off hunger in a pinch.

Two-point-nine miles up the Tote Road from Neso is a two space parking place on the left where a small routed wood sign says "Parking."

A worn trail leads into the woods for a short way before bypassing a tall earthen mound with boulders in front of it, and an old iron gate post with no gate attached. Beyond the mound, a grassy road winds into the woods, and this is the remains of the old east-west road between what's now Route 11 and the Allagash region. Edmund Ware Smith talks about driving his station wagon across this road in his fine book, *Up River and Down*, when he was making for the Allagash. It's obvious from the mowing some post of civilization is not far, and in a few minutes I emerge at the outlet dam of Nesowadnehunk Lake across from Nesowadnehunk Wilderness Campground, which looks no more like wilderness than Disney World. I'd hear the generator as soon as I get out of the car. There's a store, and a couple of dozen more or less permanently-parked campers crammed cheek by jowl into a grassy lakeside clearing. I almost turn back, but curiosity takes hold, and I walk across the dam. Halfway across the dam, there's a plaque honoring a gentleman who hand-carried five thousand fish from the stream to the lake because they wouldn't take the fish ladder. It is indeed heartening to read about this honorable deed.

The existence of this aberration of a campground five minutes from the park boundary almost defies comprehension. Convenience or curse, I'm not sure which. Inside the store, an energetic blond lady holds sway. She's from Turner and says she's up here to help out for the bear hunt. She has the deep, cracked, bronze skin of a person who's spent too much time in the sun and for whom skin cancer is a matter of time. "We spend winters in Florida. Lots of 'em here do." The store is predictable. Beer in the coolers, milk, and eggs. Circular racks of sweatshirts with writing on them. There's a table with a couple of full Crock-Pots, if you don't want to cook. Adjacent to the store there's a dining area.

"What are those birds hovering out there?" she asks.

"I don't know. I was trying to figure that out too. The light was bad." A flock of something twitters over the bridge. They come out of a stand of fir, grabbing insects out of the air.

"I think they're cedar waxwings. I'm a big birder, I've got to go out and see."

She comes out with binoculars and lights a cigarette. "Yup, cedar waxwings. I've never seen them do that. Catch bugs like that."

"Me neither. I've only seen them eat berries."

The Wilderness Campground is hard on your eyes. There's the blinding white of the plastic campers. The flotsam and jetsam of camper life piled around—grills, boats, lawn chairs, woodpiles. Outside the store and down a bank there's a dump that looks like it gets burned once in a while. A moldy upside-down La-Z-Boy resides there now, waiting for the fire. And other debris, surrounded by the strange vegetation that grows onto human disturbance. Curious what happens when man scratches the surface of the earth.

At South Branch Pond a canoe, paddle, and life preserver rent for a dollar an hour. You sign in on the front porch of the ranger station, and when you return you record your time and deposit your money into a slot in the door. Besides the racks of canoe gear, there are racks of wildlife literature, a large 3D model of the mountains surrounding the pond, and several admonitions about littering. Down at the water, bottom up on the racks, lies a fleet of green Old Town Discoveries that have seen better days. I choose the fairest one—the bottoms tend to have taken the shape of waves—put a thirty pound rock in the bow, and push off. It feels good to float, and the views from the pond are inspiring. The rocky and forested ramparts of Traveler Mountain rise dramatically from the east side of the pond. A great basin between two of Traveler's peaks recedes from the pond into the blue sky, and the sounds of Howe Brook, which drain the basin, spill across the water.

At the west end of North Pond, a brook enters from South Pond which lies a few feet higher a hundred yards away. Today the current is brisk and too shallow to paddle, so I look for a stick to use as a pole. By the time I'm equipped with a stick, a family of four in two canoes has entered the stream ahead of me, and their boats are stalled in the current. Dad and the boy get out and start dragging the canoes forward with some difficulty, while the mom and daughter remain seated, white knuckles firmly attached to the gunwales of their canoe. The dad slips and the female grips tighten.

"Why are we doing this? Why don't we just turn around?"

"Because I want to try and get somewhere," says Dad. The family canoes make slow progress, but mine is just as slow. A couple of times the current drives me against the shore, and it takes effort to coax the canoe back into the stream. The family is almost to the upper pond, when my stick snaps, and the boat spins and rushes back toward North Pond. Just as well. Let the family have their quiet time on the upper lake. Next time I'll bring a pole.

A quarter mile from the inlet, Howe Brook Trail takes off for the pools and the Lower Falls, two tenths of a mile, and to Upper Falls, two miles. I tie the canoe, shoulder the pack, and in a few minutes emerge onto ledges overlooking Howe Brooke. Strangely beautiful blue pools swirl inside bowls of smooth rock. I startle a man and a woman sitting by the water smoking, and when they see me, they both drop their cigarettes out of sight, guilty as charged. Caution: Cigarette smoking is hazardous to your health. She says hi and he does not, and I keep going along the rocks thinking how I used to be like them, hiding cigarettes, and remembering the feeling of having a smoke in a contemplative place. Smoking is a false respite now though, and all the fun is gone, because anytime you light up you know you're inhaling a little bit of death.

Howe Brook turns out to be a splendor of natural beauty. The mountains' metamorphic rock imparts a fantastic sparkling blue tint to the water. It's hard to imagine a substance more pure, and I'm sure the dozen leopard frogs I meet on the trail concur. At least I think they're leopard frogs—maybe they're pickerel frogs. It doesn't matter really—I see more frogs in a mile than I see in a couple of years anywhere else. The ground is still saturated from Irene, a tumultuous lady storm that redesigned Howe Brook's banks as she went through the neighborhood. Football-sized rocks are heaped up in new places, and storm water undercut banks and swept away chunks of earth and trees. The trail squishes and sometimes trickles. Clots of forest duff driven down the mountainside by Irene's freshets jam up against the trees. Stranded high and dry above the stream bed, driftwood driven by the maelstrom is sorted into piles by size and length.

The stream is pleasant, and the sounds of the water making way down the mountain are so elemental and affirming, but for some reason I feel like this is the longest two mile hike I've ever taken. Theorem #1 comes to mind. It's an easy grade, but again I break a sweat in the cool and humid understory. My legs suddenly remember they hiked six mountain miles yesterday, and take up a gentle but relentless protest. I check my watch but can't remember when I left the landing.

After about an hour of irrational thought hiking alone in the woods, fear kicks in. A couple of times I look over my shoulder, up steep forest slopes climbing a couple thousand feet skyward. Coyotes? Wolves? Mountain lion? Hard chance, but it would be naive to try and tell myself there's no way. Far more likely than a wild animal confrontation, a branch might drop on my head, or I might fall and sprain an ankle, something I've never done. Am I prepared to spend the night in the woods? Not at all. At least not comfortably, and if something did happen and I couldn't get out on my own, it would be dark before a search started. They would find the canoe eventually, and have several miles of trails to search. Stay on the trail. Stay on the trail. Stay on the trail.

Long after it feels like I should have reached the falls, the trail turns steep. Fifty feet to the right the stream, which has shrunk as I've ascended past the half dozen feeder brooks, seethes through a chasm, a white aerated strand in free fall. I get off the trail to investigate this mossy, green Eden, fifty-foot rock walls over arched by tree canopy, the roiling water and the dripping air, a lair of lichens that never see sun.

On the way back to the pond, I investigate the woodpiles deposited by the storm. I pick up a baseball-sized burl, smooth as a stone, and a couple of stone-rubbed sticks all rounded like they've been tumbled. The three sculptures are saturated with water, but by the time I get them home, cracks have started to open into their interiors.

Ice Out Trip on Lobster Lake

All winter the rebuilt canoe and I yearn to get out on the water early in the spring. Ice out dates in Maine lakes are newsworthy events, and have been recorded for Moosehead Lake since 1848[1]. Going by historical data, a trip during the last week in April looks like a good chance, but by May 7, 2010, ice on Moosehead and most Maine lakes has been history for a month. As a trip to the woods gets close, I check the seven-day weather forecasts several times a day. This is not the first time the forecasts have gone downhill the closer the time comes. Wind, rain, temperatures in the 30s. A good chance of snow, sleet, and freezing rain during the latter part of my trip. A last check on the weather confirms ice may be out of the lakes, but not out of the air yet, and at the last minute I reserve a cabin at Loon Lodge for a couple of nights when the weather is predicted to be the worst.

It takes most of a day to sort out gear and pack it into the Pathfinder. There's more stuff than I thought, but then this happens every time. You can't travel light and bring along cast iron frying pans. I am culture-bound to the iron pans in the same way that Franklin Expedition sailors took the ship's silver flatware with them onto the ice when they abandoned ship, as if a silver spoon was the only way to eat.

The 1907 Old Town Charles River canoe rides on the roof. This will be my first trip in the canoe, which is coming out of a five year renovation. The work included stripping off the old fiberglass (the result of a previous renovation), stripping paint and varnish from the interior,

---

1 The trend on average is toward an earlier ice out; from 1848 until now we have added about a six day increase to the navigable water's time.

repairing rotten stems, replacing decks and rails, and new layers of epoxy and cloth. Progress came in fits and starts. It took ten times longer to scrape the old varnish out of the inside than it took the factory to build the canoe in the first place. I often wondered if it was worth it, and more than once thought about dragging it out to the burn pile. Appreciation of the sweet lines and respect for the materials kept me from abandoning ship, though. The frames and planks are original, the latter of old growth fir probably sawed from three hundred year old trees. It is Old Town Canoe #6414—the number stamped into the stems. I have copies of the original sales order. The boat was started on March 14, 1907, and two days later it was canvassed. On May 7 it was shipped to Mr. Charles Smith via St Paul's School's Barn, Concord, NH. It cost thirty dollars.

Steady showers fall out of gloomy gray skies as I head up Route 15 north of Bangor, through Maine's back forty of run-down farm country, the depleted mill town of Dover Foxcroft, and Monson, the slate town where the Appalachian Trail heads into Maine's Hundred Mile Wilderness. In Greenville I stop at the Maine Guide and Tackle Shop to fill some gaps in my fishing kit. The store is a quiet, reverent place, more sanctuary than store, with wonderful wooden cases stocked with colorful flies and streamers, fly rods hanging on the walls, and shelves of books. It's almost as good as fishing. I tell the gentleman I have no idea what I'm doing, and he takes me around and picks out eight feathery and thready creations. I tell him I'm going up to Lobster, and he recommends a streamer that will imitate a smelt at the mouth of the stream, and then, for the West Branch, another fly. In no time I've spent thirty dollars, and I wonder how many sunken logs my new flies will catch for me. I forget the names immediately, but later looking back at the website I find more flies to buy. It wouldn't matter that you didn't know when to tie on a Maple Syrup, a Royal Coachman, a Grey or a Blue Ghost, because with company like that who needs a fish.

North out of Greenville, up the east side of Moosehead toward Kokadjo on the Lily Bay Road. The *Maine Atlas and Gazetteer* is open on the passenger seat, and I follow my progress north, watching the car's compass and checking off the myriad brooks, ponds, bridges, big turns and side roads. For a few miles the road skirts the lake and the necklace of homely camps strung along the shore, and then after Kokadjo you feel like you're in the woods. A couple of young moose shuffle through a parking area. Some Canada Geese are holed up in a beaver flowage, and a pair of kingfishers swoops along the trees lining a pond.

The Lily Bay Road turns into the Silas Hill Road, and then when it feels high time for it, Silas Hill road joins the Golden Road, the famous North Woods logging superhighway that runs from Millinocket east to the Canadian border. The parking area where Lobster Stream enters the West Branch is puddled and slick and deserted. Thunder rolls in the western sky. I am reluctant to pack the canoe and start out in a thunderstorm, so I drive a couple miles further west to Northeast Carry, the centuries-old canoe route between Moosehead Lake and the West Branch of the Penobscot.

Today the carry is a straight, single-track gravel road. It's not so popular a canoe route as it was in the 19th century, when Moosehead Lake was one of the major routes into the woods for loggers, sportsmen, and recreational canoeists. Mr. Thoreau passed over the carry a couple of times. Photographs of the day show horse-drawn wagons piled with a dozen canoes. Now the network of woods roads allows vehicle access to scores of put-ins north of Moosehead, and the carry has been bypassed. The distance I've just driven in two hours would have taken two days in a canoe, a fact that saddens me a little, because I know my experience to be diminished in more ways than only time.

A hamlet of forlorn buildings sags into the lay of the land. Raymond's, The Store with so Much More, is boarded up. In the winter Raymond's caters to snowmobilers and feeds a herd of deer. Online Raymond's offers "Free Advise", (*sic*) and also groceries, beer, chips, flat tire repair, and a couple of cabins for rent. At the lake's edge, I see thousands of ancient travelers disembarking from their canoes and unloading their gear onto the shore. The lake water is gray and rough, windblown like the sky clouds flowing from the west. Raindrops splatter into the puddles. The gray clay slurry of the Golden Road is splattered all over the car, and far off in the western sky is a bright blue glimmer. A break is coming. It's a splashy slog back over the Stream Road, an old corduroy road coming apart at the seams. They built corduroy roads in low-lying wet areas by laying down a base of logs perpendicular to the direction of road like a log raft, then dumped gravel over the top. Without the logs for support, a vehicle would drive gravel down into the muck and disappear. If a corduroy road is in good repair, you don't know the logs are there, but here many logs jut toward the sky and must be driven around. In some places crews have pulled out an errant log, cast it aside and filled the hole in with stone. Ten miles per hour is plenty fast over this road, and I'm thankful for the high clearance of the Pathfinder.

The gray snarl of the next squall already smudges the horizon by the time I push off from the landing, and half a mile upstream thunder cracks over my head and sends me to the bank. I tuck a tarp over the canoe and myself, and watch from under a spruce tree as first rain, then a fusillade of hail pelt the river. A few minutes later, the blue sky is back, the squall lumbering away to the east like a retreating animal.

The elevations of Lobster Lake and the West Branch of the Penobscot are so close that when water is up in the river, the current in Lobster Stream reverses and flows toward the lake. That was the case one time in the river drive era when a log boss unfamiliar with the river took a wrong turn and drove his logs "down" Lobster Stream and into the lake instead of down the Penobscot. The story has it that it took the crew a summer to round up the logs and herd them back into the Penobscot.

The banks along the stream are low and molded out of blue clay thick with alders and marsh grass. Several large elms tower over the thickets. You think of elms as a town tree offering shade, and they look strange growing solitary in the Maine woods. Maybe these elms are resistant to disease, or maybe the pernicious beetles don't survive this far north. Under one elm's canopy, I espy an American Bittern a few feet from the stream bank. The big bird is tall and brown like the grasses, and slinks away from the water into a screen of vegetation. He freezes like a stone with his long bill pointed straight up, and had I not seen his movement a few seconds before, I never would have picked him out of his camouflage.

A mile later the stream makes a right angle turn between low-lying banks of puckerbrush, and suddenly the panorama of Lobster Lake and the surrounding mountains opens up. The gale of wind whipping down the miles-long fetch of the lake gives me a shiver. The water I see is a frothing, boiling, wind-driven taupe maelstrom nothing like the flat blue waters I've studied on paper for several years. Out in the middle, water and sky merge in a foamy tempest, and it's sure no place for a canoe. By good fortune my course toward Shallow Bay campsite lies in the lee of the west shore, and in a foot of water I make way over a lovely expanse of clean sand.

An expansive moose land lies on the other side of a kind of barrier beach. At first I take the alder-crowned berm separating lake from bog as a natural geologic formation, but then realize the mile-long formation is a beaver dam. The water on the other side is two feet higher than the lake water. In several spots water spills out of the pond and scours a deep channel into the lake bottom.

I don't see any moose, but I feel them everywhere. Their tracks pock the soft sand. They've scraped so much bark off the trees that a bright swath of cambium overlays the bog like a layer of yellow mist. Red-winged blackbirds light among the branches of cambium and call shrill notes. A large flock of another bird I can't identify swoops over the lake, feasting on a hatch of something.

A small sign with routed lettering stained an unobtrusive brown designates Shallow Bay Campsite. It's a bony place on a skinny point of land, with not a lot of trees between it and the wetland where the north wind is in charge. There's not a lot of choice. Going further means more exposure to wind and increased chance of getting pinned down. So I set up, make a fire out of wet wood, and cook dinner. In the wind, the fire affords little warmth beyond the circumference of the ring, so I crawl into the tent early. A full gale speeds by not far overhead, hissing through the tossing branches, and making so much noise a sound sleep is a remote possibility. A night is a long time to consider the ways a tree might come down and make trouble for me. No trees fall at Shallow Bay that night, but in the next several days I come across dozens of downed trees in the roads.

Friday morning temperatures are in the thirties, and the wind blows the lake into an inhospitable spume. The coffee takes forever to perk in my new Chinese coffee pot, but finally coffee and I discuss the situation while bacon and eggs sputter in the cast iron pan. With weather like this, it makes no sense to go further down the lake, and we decide to move over to the West Branch, where the sheltered river waters will be friendlier to the canoe.

The wind careens offshore 45 degrees to my paddling angle, and the waters of Shallow Bay really are shallower than the depth of the paddle blade, so I walk the canoe back to the stream. It follows like a good dog, only gently tugging on the rope leash four feet downwind, while I slosh along in a few inches of water. Where leaks in the bog have scoured out the channels, I put one foot in the canoe, shove off, and glide to the other side to resume the watery hike. Halfway to the outlet, I pull the canoe in to shore, hunker down in the windbreak of a large jack pine root ball, and heat up coffee left over from breakfast. Forty miles east, Katahdin looms in spring plumage—her broad flanks dappled green and black like the back of a mackerel. Soon the white snowfields gathered at the peaks will molt, and the mountain's summer feathers will emerge to fly over the North Country.

There is no sign of the bittern on the return trip, and no sign of much else either, until I round a bend and see a motorboat approaching. A man in oilskins stands lookout in the bow, and when he sees me he signals the helmsman to slow down. Before long we are broadside to one another, and the lookout calls, "That is a fine looking canoe." He emphasizes the word *fine*.

"Thanks," I say and wave back. There's nothing like a boat compliment to make a guy feel good. A mountain of gear heaps over the rails of the skiff. There are no concerns about traveling light for that expedition, no doubt equipped with a full set of cast iron frying pans.

At Lobster Landing, I find the population has boomed overnight. Six pickup trucks hooked to boat trailers keep the Pathfinder company, but my fine looking canoe and I don't stop. We slip under the new steel bridge and a minute later we're drifting down the West Branch of the Penobscot.

This West Branch rises west of here near Canada, flows easterly over the top of Moosehead Lake (which lies in the Kennebec River Watershed), down to Chesuncook Lake (created out of three small lakes by Ripogenous Dam), then on to Millinocket and many more dams to a rendezvous with the East Branch in Medway. The Penobscot Watershed drains a third of Maine's land.

Besides being a natural treasure, the river also flows with centuries of rich human history, and it's impossible not to feel the history as the canoe and I drift downriver through the aisles of fir and pine. The region has been home to Wabanaki peoples for close to ten thousand years, and they are a strong presence on the river today. The Penobscots own all the islands in the river below Medway, and inhabit Indian Island in Old Town. Early in the 17th century, European trappers and lumbermen moved into the woods, and by the middle of the 19th century, lumber barons controlled most of the Maine North Woods, and the forest fell to meet the world's appetite for lumber products. That legacy pretty much shapes the character of the woods today—a working forest with generous access extended to the public. In the late 20th century, log transport switched to trucks operating on thousands of miles of dirt roads. Recreation became the major activity on the Penobscot.

A mile downriver from where Lobster Stream lets in, the Golden Road crosses the West Branch over a bridge called Hannibal's Crossing. A huge yellow grader emerges from the woods and drags a mucous gray cloud of road dust across the bridge. It's a strange intrusion into the river world, and a harsh reminder of industry close at hand. A mile further lies Warren Island, or Thoreau Island as it is known today—because Henry camped there in 1853 and 1857. The island is my destination now.

The river is hugely pleasant to be on this morning. Overhead the strident winds still course from the west, but here the sun warms the air and illuminates the river water with forest reflections. Sometimes the wind dips down and sweeps a frond of ripples across the surface, but most of the time it's like black glass, a mill pond dimpled by a sleepy knot-and-a-half current. Several mergansers' brilliant white breasts glow iridescent in the dark coniferous shadows along the river bank. At one point I join up with a muskrat headed downriver, and we keep company for a while, he slightly in the lead about ten feet off the port bow. I'm surprised how tolerant he is of me. It's hard to believe, but these critters have a reputation as a fine entree on the North Woods menu. Early woodsmen shot a lot of his kin for camp food, as did the Indians who called them musquash.

The campsite at Thoreau Island occupies a high prow of land in a grassy clearing with a fine view upriver. The ground has a scrubbed clean feeling, and I notice grass and debris snagged in branches three feet off the ground. The spring floods washed over this place and spiffed things up after last year's wear and tear. There's no question I'm the first human visitor of 2010.

I'd worried a small island might be pretty well picked over for firewood, and am relieved to find that not the case. Except for the campsite area, the island is heavily wooded, and much standing and fallen dead wood lies close to camp. A trail leads away down island, first passing the outhouse, then petering out in the woods among spruce and pine. Most of the trees on the island are small. Only a handful of big cedars and one large pine stand down at the east end. The pine is undoubtedly more than a hundred and fifty years old, so it stood when Thoreau was here. I give the pine a pat, feeling the presence of the famous visitor across the decades.

More recent visitors to the island have left piles of calling cards on the pine needle carpet. One wonders about the attractions of a small island for moose, but almost nothing in the woods presents an obstacle to moose. Island, mountaintop, middle of a pond, it's all the same to them—one terrain as negotiable as another with four legs six feet long, and an affinity for water. After all, their diet is trees, and trees are everywhere in the Maine woods.

As night flows downstream over the island, there is not much to do but crawl into the tent and into the sleeping bag. The river glides by me without so much as a murmur, though I can feel the current through the dark. Late at night a strange, plaintive call from across the river wakes me: *woni woni woni, woni woni woni*. I don't know what it is, but it's not something with fangs, so I am more curious than edgy. Mostly it reminds me how much I don't know. Later, close to dawn, large wings flap low over the tent. An owl, perhaps, or an eagle patrolling the river. I'm up at 5:00 A.M. in time to see the stars waning, and with them the last of the clear sky. True to forecast, a precipitous grayness looms in the west.

There's no rush to break camp. My cabin reservations are at Loon Lodge, a sporting camp only a couple hours drive north from Lobster Landing. As usual, coffee trumps all other morning activities, including the first daylight whizz. This morning I discover a new ritual while watching the coffee start to perk. Without thinking about it, I pour some of the hot brown liquid onto a towel and wash my face with fresh coffee.

Early Spring in the Allagash Woods

After two blustery days of paddling and camping by the water, the log cabin feels like heaven. The construction is tight, and the wood stove easily handles the spring chills. By traditional Maine woods standards, this cabin is luxurious—it's got an ample front porch with firewood stacked across the front. Inside a stuffed chair stands in a corner with a lamp that's plugged into the cabin's only receptacle, and which I can turn on during generator hours. There's also a sofa, not so comfortable as the chair, a dining set, counter with sink, and an apartment-sized gas stove. There's a separate sleeping room with a double bed, a bunk bed, and one small window. Nights in the sleeping room are black as pitch. I am very happy to be here, though a voice from the wilderness now and then calls to tell me I wimped out on the camping trip, and really I should be hunkered somewhere on the lake trying to stay warm and dry. It's still raining outside, and the temperature is in the 30s, but with the promise of a warm cabin to come back to, the prospect of getting soaked in the woods doesn't bother me. Allagash Lake is three miles up the Carry Road, a drivable stretch, but I set out for the lake on foot.

The Carry Road climbs up through a cut-over forest traced with mazes of skidder roads. The woods have been growing back for twenty years, but the twitching roads are still prominent, thick with raspberries. In flat, featureless country these skidder roads can turn a person around faster than a top. Today I am not tempted, though I do wander alongside the road looking for shed moose antlers. Sign is everywhere. The saplings are browsed back, pom-pom droppings are fresh, and water-filled tracks pock the soaked ground. It feels like I'm standing in the mooses' living room.

In moose woods I keep in mind a plan of action, should a meeting go the wrong way. It's contrary to all my experience in the woods, but the archetypal image of the charging bull moose is a hard thing to disregard. It's not rutting season, but a mother with calf would be just as dangerous. Everyone but the red squirrels go in the opposite direction as quickly as possible without stopping to ask questions, the bears quickest of all. I'm not sure who's more timid, the animals or me, but I know they all run faster. Still, a moose meeting would be a welcome event, and the chance of one keeps me on my toes.

Halfway to the lake, the Carry Road swings wide to the west and slopes down into a swamp. Through the woods at the far end of the curve, I suddenly spy a large moose walking toward me on the road, head down, quite lost in moose thoughts. He sees me seconds after I see him, unfortunately, because I would have liked to observe his pensive and amiable expression for longer. Alas, I startle him, or we startle each other, and he rears his head at the same time his front feet skid to a stop. He bucks around like a bronco at a rodeo and gallops away back the way he'd come. My reaction is similar. Recoiling at the sight of him and his abrupt movement, I sidestep right to begin a retreat. I look over my shoulder and see him leaving at the same time he looks over his shoulder at me. However, in the time I move three feet he covers one hundred, and in no time he melts into the dense foliage of the cedar swamp. I look and listen for him where he disappeared—but nothing is revealed and it's as if he never existed.

The May rains patter down through the unfurling foliage in a chilly slur. The clouds press close, the clayey ground wheezles under my boots. The road fords a beaver pond where the fine rain seethes on the water. The rain runs down my jacket and drips onto my jeans, making me wetter below the waist than if I wore no jacket. I don't mind getting wet. It makes me feel at home in the cold spring woods; besides, there's a warm cabin at the end of the day.

A rugged steel gate a mile from the lake defines the limit of vehicle access. No motorized vehicles beyond the yellow gate, and no motorboats on the lake either. (Most of the Allagash Waterway is open to motorboats, but not Allagash Lake). The old road continues, though, and with a canoe carrier it's an easy portage from the parking area at the gate to the lake. A half mile from the lake, the Carry Trail separates from the road, constricts to a narrow hiking trail, and descends toward the lake along a path choked with rocks and roots. The trail crosses a brook, filled more with black mossy rocks than water, then a stand of big hemlocks that block so much light that day turns to night. It's here you first glimpse the gleam of the lake through the trees—and then suddenly, in the abrupt way things can happen in the woods, the trail emerges from the forest beside the wide lake, its water like polished pewter and mutely shimmering in the mists.

From here the lake stretches five miles north, surrounded on all sides by miles of northern forest. From east to west it's three miles across at the widest point. Pine, cedar, spruce, and hemlock stand down to the shore. Already shadows are thickening the gray skies. I waited until late in the afternoon to walk up here, and as if serving notice, a breeze scudding off the water chills me. I turn away from the waters and start walking home. I am reluctant to leave, but look forward to the warm glow of the cabin, the soft chair, and a cup of tea. The Maine woods are a wonderful place to be when you're in a warm place.

More rain in the morning. The thermometer on the porch says 36 degrees. I brew coffee, cook bacon and oatmeal, stoke the fire, make more coffee. I write in my notebooks in the quiet before generator time which starts at 8:00 A.M. When it does start, I get up and putter with cabin chores. Heat water for dishes, fill the wood box, fill the water jugs, sweep the floor and porch.

By early afternoon I feel cabin-bound and am eager to return to the lake. This time I drive up to the gate and stay straight on the old road until coming out at the ranger station in a small clearing beside the lake. A large motorized canoe rests on the shore, but the cabin looks empty and quiet. It's a substantial structure and well-equipped. There are two solar panels on the roof, an outhouse two hundred feet away, and several cords of firewood stacked under tarps.

Right where I think it should be, I find the Allagash Mountain Trail at the north end of the clearing. The trail begins a gentle but steady ascent through a mixed open forest where white and red trillium bloom among last year's brown leaves. Their leaves are stark and lovely and feel very tenuous in such vast and unfeeling woods. This trail is in the lee of the westerlies which still buffet the land after three days. The wind scours the mountaintop above me, but here the new green pig's ear leaves only tremble.

Half a mile in, the trail gets steeper, rockier, and slipperier, and the higher I climb the stronger the wind blows. When I emerge from the small stunted spruces onto the exposed ledges of the summit, the rain starts to freeze. It's a raw world, gray green and wet as far as you can see in all directions.

Smack on top of Allagash Mountain stands an abandoned fire tower. It's a square hut perched high over the rocks on an erector set frame, and the steel cables anchoring it to the rock make a mournful instrument in the wind. I waste no thoughts on climbing the skeleton ladder that disappears into the dark abdomen of the tower. Cold sleet stabs my bare face. The big block of Allagash Lake lies couched in the forest below, and beyond the lake the far reaching waters of the Allagash region merge with the mists. The green forest stains the sky green. The lonely beauty of spring on the mountaintop sinks in, but I don't stay long. Starting down I find that broken rocks and krummholz obscure the beginning of the trail, and I pause for a moment, thinking how not a soul in the whole wide world knows where I am.

Halfway out the Carry Trail, I meet Jay the ranger pushing a cart loaded with supplies toward his cabin. It's the beginning of the season, and he's getting set up for his first nine-day stay. "Nine days on, five off," he says. In the cart are his chain saw and a dry bag filled with clothes. He took food in a couple of days ago. He's got a wide, open, tanned face, red beard, knee-high green rubber boots, two or three shirts, the outer one unbuttoned, and a friendly manner. He tells me he has just been visiting Loon Lodge where I am staying.

"They are good, friendly folks," I say.

"Got to be," he says, matter-of-factly, as if there's no choice. "Don't know when you're going to need help." I ask him if the lake gets crowded in the summer, or if you can usually find a camping spot. "You usually can," he says. "It's a big square lake. You've got to watch the wind. Waves out in the middle can get like this." He holds his hand about thirty inches from the ground. I say the Carry Trail looks like a rugged piece to carry a canoe over.

"Oh, people bring their canoes in and launch right in front of my place. The key is to travel light."

"I like my cast iron pans."

"Make two trips then." Right, it is that simple after all. He says in about an hour he'll have his fire going and supper on the stove. "I think tonight it's going to be a can of something, but I've got some peppers and onions to make it better." I believe I will have something out of a can myself. We are both looking forward to warm cabins. I tell him I am envious of his. "I've probably got the best spot in the woods," he says, and pushes off toward the lake. I head back to my cabin in the woods where my time is winding down. I'll be heading out in the morning.

Back at Loon Lodge I go find Ray and Leslie to say thank you and goodbye. They are at home above the main lodge, where they have an apartment. I tell them I'll be leaving early, going out on the Millinocket side. After chatting for a while, I ask Ray if he knows of wolves in the Maine woods. Before he speaks, I see him turning the question over in his mind, which I infer to mean there's more than one way to answer the question, depending who you're talking to.

"If there were wolves in these woods it would put some things off limits for some people." That's not a yes, and it's not a no, but I interpret it to be more in the affirmative than not. I say that coyotes have interbred with the wolves, and so the distinction between coyote, which are common if not infrequently seen, and wolf, which are more secretive and seldom seen, is blurry. "Mike and I were riding one day and we saw a huge coyote. Mike said he'd never seen one so big. Now that makes you wonder." It does make you wonder.

The wonder and mystery of the woods dwell deep in the dark northern nights. Here an unfathomable dream world slides past, like a panorama of moving forest filled with beneficent creatures. The spirit world pulsates close by—at night it is so thick it feels almost tangible, yet you cannot touch it. It's a world as old as man and where our oldest companions live. In the light of day, the night world recedes like an invisible star.

Mists, Mosquitoes, and Things like Bateaux

We are five paddlers in three canoes drifting out of the somnolent waters of Lobster Stream into the more assertive current of the West Branch. It's been raining for most of the past twenty-four hours, and it's raining now. I watch the drops plash on the glossy river. A drop dents the water, and then the pewter bead skitters sideways on the surface before pausing and popping and merging with the big flow of the river. If we had a choice, we would have chosen a sunny day for this trip, and I would not be out here watching the rain. Yet here we are surrounded by all this beauty. I reach out and it touches me. Such a simple thing, rain falling on the river.

We are coming off two nights camping on Ogden Point at Lobster Lake. Ogden Point looks like a tropical beach of paradise dropped into the middle of the Maine woods—its fine white sands lovely and inviting, and home to a number of very large jack pines, a rare conifer in Maine. From the point which separates Shallow Bay from the Claw Bays, there is a stunning vista of Big Spenser Mountain twelve miles away. It's a long squarish mountain with a flat top and pleasant blue sides, and from Ogden a pleasing backdrop to the many islands filling the Claw Bays.

The wonderful fine white sand of Ogden Point, which the boys take to in bare feet with gusto, quickly loses my admiration as the substance sticks to our feet and every item of gear, and begins to accumulate in the tents, in the canoes, on the picnic table, and to infiltrate every pocket and sock, every pan and pot. The boys don't seem to mind, but Holly and I try to manage the impact. At best the battle of the sands is a draw.

At dusk the mosquitoes introduce themselves in droves, an occurrence the boys counter by applying half a spray can of Off! onto their exposed skin, which is most of their bodies. I put on more shirts and gather materials for a smudge fire to light in our cast iron pot. Some birch bark, jack pine cones, and some pitchy pine knots flare up and send a plume of rank gray smoke swirling under the tarp, and soon the mosquitoes decide to relocate.

The rain starts falling during the first night of the trip and falls intermittently the next three days. It makes the world drippy and damp, and some spirits soggy and unsmiling. Our two- night stay at Ogden Point Sands was designed to lessen camp setup and breakdown time and to increase time for fishing and cooking and reading. It works for a while, but in an unexpected way the delay puts the essence of the trip on hold. The waiting feeds our wanderlust for the river, our appetite for movement, and the craving of unfolding journey. The crew is antsy to get going this morning, which is as it should be, but we break no records for breaking camp. By the time we've cooked the last of our bacon and eggs, cleaned dishes, rinsed the sand out of the canoes, packed up two tents, personal gear, our substantial kitchen, and the flotsam of fishing gear, day packs, and odds and ends, two hours have elapsed. It's mid-morning before we bid the point goodbye. I was glad to have been there once, but would not return if there's a choice. Give me a camp under soughing pines anytime. Leave the beaches at the ocean. A brisk east wind licks the lake. We stick close to shore heading for Lobster Stream, which from most of the lake is hidden among the low grassy banks. It takes only a few minutes to cross the shallow bay.

Holly is in the bow of our canoe, a sixteen-foot plank-on-frame and clear-coated Prospector I built in our garage. The canoe's rocker and arch hull give it a quick motion, and every move we make translates into canoe movement. We might have been better off in a more stable canoe for her first trip, but I hope the canoe will be more comfortable when we start to paddle better as a team.

My son Mariner and his friend Gavin are paddling the Old Town 174 Discovery, a faded red—I can't call it pink—ABS canoe, looking very down-at-the-heels after years of bottom-up outside storage. To get the canoe ready for the trip, I got out a heat gun and finished peeling off the decals the sun had started. Then with a hose I washed off forest life that had found a home between the hull and the gunwale. I bought this canoe for two hundred and fifty dollars at the Old Town factory, back when Old Town still had a soul. It wasn't the boat I really wanted—but it was all I could afford, a factory second because of a few square inches of bubbly texture in the bottom. It's made from an early generation of ABS, the stuff that deforms when exposed to too much sun, and I noticed while loading it on the trailer that the bottom has a serious hog, a deformity I hoped would go away when the canoe was loaded and floating. From what I can see that didn't happen. It never was a very good-looking canoe, and it doesn't look good now.

Abe's paddling the 1907 Old Town Charles River. He wanted to try some solo paddling this trip, and the Charles River is perfect for one person and some gear. I bought the canoe for a hundred dollars, stripped off the old varnish and polyester resins and glass, and clear-coated the hull with epoxy. The planking and frames are almost all original—I had to replace some short pieces of planks at the ends and replace the top several inches of the stems, both rotten where the boat had been stored upside down on the ground. It's a sweet, venerable canoe. Its old growth planking and frames are likely four hundred years old.

So far the rain has made itself the main distraction of the trip. This morning we packed up in the rain, and we're paddling in the rain. Holly is soaked and unhappy, and that makes me reluctant to say I'm having a good time. The sounds of the showers falling on the river are rhythmic and peaceful.

I am not wearing rain gear, but a lightweight fast-drying pair of pants that keep water out for a while. Now and then a few drops coalesce on the inside and run a cool trickle down my thigh into the nether regions of my crotch. It's disconcerting but not too uncomfortable. The way you get through this kind of weather is to merge with it if you can, be wet and appreciate the world is wet, and you are a little piece at home in the wet world. I dare say nothing to my boat mate, miserable and mute in the bow. After two days in the woods I'm smoky, sweaty, soaked, and approaching equilibrium with the woods. It's just the kind of feeling that draws me here.

A mile below our joining the West Branch, we slip under Hannibal's Bridge and the Golden Road, and soon after pass Thoreau Island, a sliver of an island where I have stayed before. Then we enter the Moosehorn Deadwater, several miles of sluggish river flanked with conifers greenly effervescent under the drippy gray sky. From within the fir and spruce spires issue the operatic warbles of the white-throated sparrows, their clairvoyant songs spilling back and forth across the river from forested minarets. It somehow feels like their voices are amplified in the rain. We disturb an eagle several times, meet two families of Canada Geese hunkered down on the shore, and bother several merganser moms and their ducklings who try mightily to maintain the maximum distance from the canoes without leaving the river. A headwind springs up along the Moosehorn's straightaways, and when we stop paddling for water and a snack late in the morning, the canoes hesitate, then edge back upstream a bit.

We have in mind to stop at Big Island and camp on the bluff that overlooks the river. The woodsy site under the tall soughing pines would be a welcome contrast to the sands of Ogden Point, but alas, when the island hoves into view, three canoes are nuzzling its shore.

"First come, first served," I say for no reason. "It's who starts out on the river earliest gets their choice of sites." The boys have lingered at Little Ragmuff half a mile upriver, trying out the fishing. Holly and I drift around in circles waiting for them, contemplating our next move, when a white-bearded, hatted man calls out from the island, "Does that canoe have frames?"

"Yes, it does," I say. He's asking because clear-finished canoes are most often strip-built, a rugged but lowly method of construction, most often utilized by do-it-yourself canoe builders. I'm a do- it-yourselfer but steered away from the strip-built method because I don't like the aesthetics of it.

"Bring it in here so I can see it, and I'll show you our kitchen."

Fair enough. He clomps down the stairs cut into the bluff, talking as he comes, and as we sidle into the shore, he asks me what the black material on the canoe's rails is.

"Pipe insulation," I say, and he says, "Hmmf," and that seems to be the end of the canoe side of the conversation. Next it's our turn to clomp up the stairs and view the camp kitchen, a workmanlike plywood box with lots of cubbies and shelf space standing on spindly legs that retract into compartments in the box. A lid on hinges folds down level to make a counter. I express genuine admiration for the kitchen, having made one myself—though much less sophisticated and even awkward to use—save that it's a place where all things kitchen go. My camp kitchen is like a child's toy box. You can fit lots of stuff in, but finding something you want is a challenge.

"Little Ragmuff is the best site below here, but I can't say it will be empty. There was another group ahead of us—they could be there. The one below the island is nice, not the one on the island, but the one on the left bank." The gentleman leading this Boy Scout trip is experienced and offers lots of advice.

We're in a bit of a pickle. If we pass up the site below the island and go on to Little Ragmuff and it's taken, the next site, Pine Stream, is below the flowage of the river and feels like part of the lake. We want to spend one night at least beside the trilling river, fall asleep on the bosom of its soulful song. Could there be a better bedtime story?

There's still no sign of the boys after our visit ashore. As Holly and I drop down the current on the south side of the island, I look over my shoulder often, not liking the feeling that comes when the boys are out of sight for long. They are still boys, after all, and I am responsible for their welfare during this trip, a fact that informs my orientation to the river and waters. We stop to check the campsite at the south end of Big Island. There's no landing, really, a sliver of bare bank with the current jostling against some rocks. It's inviting, but not a place to take out three canoes and set up two tents, so we drift down half a stone's throw to Smarts, a one-party site on top of a grassy bank. Thinking about making camp in a field of tall wet grass dampens the river spirits some, but there's not much choice, and when the boys finally show up, that's what we do.

The grass and overhanging boughs are soaked and dripping, the sky drips, but Smarts overlooks the river in a nice way, and there's just enough room to plant two tents in the clearing without much fuss. We stretch the tarp over the pole, and immediately the mosquitoes gather underneath to get out of the rain. The boys rig up to fish again, and I look for wood to start a fire. A well-traveled pine needle path recedes into tall woods which give the illusion of being drier than the rest of the world. Firewood scavengers have picked the ground clean of every stick for a good ways, lending it a managed, park-like aspect. I walk back there without making a sound, and in the rain gather an armload of tinder, birch bark, and dead spruce branches.

On the way back to camp, I discover an old bateau hiding under the low boughs of a pine, and stop to study it. The Maine woods and waters are filled with artifacts of the lumbering era, but most of what you find are iron objects; a length of chain, a spike, and the remains of a wooden boat are a rare thing. There's not much left of this one. A few rotted planks still tacked together with metal patches hold enough shape to define one end of the bateau, the fine angle of the bow rising in the meekest way out of its pine needle grave. Most of the boat has melted into the forest, and where the rest of the boat should be, there is only a smooth carpet of pine needles. Most likely the men who left it here are long gone to their own graves, and in the gentle rain sifting down through the forest, I wonder who they were.

The boys, undeterred by the rain, set up their tent, throw their sand-stuck gear inside, and head for the river with their fishing rods. Mariner and Abe fly fish, Gavin uses spinning gear. He's happy with his tackle, a "gold thingy with three green thingies" he bought in Greenville. He catches more fish than the other two, but they're more fun to watch, their gold lines arcing graceful curves over the dark waters. I'm content to watch the boys. When Abe decides he wants to fish close to a big rock on the other side of the river, he swims across with his rod clenched in his teeth. When they catch a fish, they reel it in, and when it's close enough to handle, they drop their fishing rod to the bottom of the river so both hands are available to release the fish.

"Number seventeen," says Abe.

"Number twenty-eight," says Gavin.

"This one is pretty big. I wonder if I should keep it, "says Mariner. I caught one fish at Lobster and that feels like enough. The river is shallow here, and warm, and there's no chance for a brook trout which might inspire me. The boys don't seem to care what kind of fish they catch.

Rain patters on the tent all night, and at dawn I get up in the rain, make coffee, and start the smudge pot. For two hours I tend the fire and watch the rain drip off the tarp into a water bucket. The sun gives subtle notice of appearing, but we break camp in showers and once more get on the river in the rain. In the few miles it takes to reach Chesuncook, blue sky begins to prevail at the same time thunderheads rumble ominously in the west. Just like that, we find ourselves abroad on the lake, the river part of the trip over, and a somewhat anticlimactic feeling beginning to creep in.

We settle in at Gero Island #2, a nice site with grand views up and down the lake. Gero Island is public reserve land with several stands of old growth trees spread around it. One could spend a week just exploring the island. Our campsite lies directly across from Chesuncook Village, a remote Maine woods destination that has eluded me for over thirty years. The recent improvements to a year-round road have diminished its reputation in my own mind, as has the sometimes contentious ownership of the famous Lake House, a proud white farmhouse dating from the mid 19th century logging heyday. With binoculars I pick out our car and trailer parked on the inn's lawn. From the vicinity of Graveyard Point, the sounds of a riding lawn mower blow across the lake and corrupt the wilderness ambiance.

I try to ignore these sights and sounds of civilization—after all, they are small features in so many miles of forest—but nonetheless, I feel the wilderness essence slipping away. It makes you wonder—if one lawn mower a mile away has such an effect, then what happens to us when a city full of contrived sights and sounds smothers our senses? I work on diverting these thoughts by tending the fire, watching the weather, and scanning the lake for canoes.

The waterfront campsite affords spectacular views but also exposes us to the wind, persistent enough to be a nuisance and also enough of a factor to make a leisurely paddle around the island impossible. The boys seem to have reached some kind of saturation point themselves, and pass several hours of the afternoon playing President with a deck of cards—the closest thing to electronic media available. Holly scores a huge culinary success at dinner, cooking cornbread from scratch in the iron frying pan over the fire.

That night the boys stay up late playing cards and eating chocolate, and in the morning Mariner emerges feeling sick to his stomach, complaining about chills and lack of sleep. It would be several doctors' visits and days later before he would be diagnosed with mono, and receive dire warnings to desist from contact sports lest some jolt rupture his red-blood-cell-engorged spleen and result in death. But meanwhile, his dreary demeanor and obvious discomfort clinch the decision to head home a day earlier than planned, and we pack up under the first sunny skies we've had. Chesuncook is only a mile paddle across the lake, fortunately the wind is down, and after twenty minutes paddling, our canoes scrape the beach below the inn.

We make a quick job of packing the trailer and take a few minutes to explore the village. There's a small building with a "For Sale" sign just up the road, and we walk up there to peek into a fir bead-board kitchen with a hand pump next to the sink. Even the boys are impressed with its "originalness," which also manifests in droopy roof lines and soft-looking floors sagging close to the damp earth. A small shack about eight-foot square near the landing is the Chesuncook Fire Department, so says the painted lettering on the door, and an investigation inside reveals a disconsolately corroded pump with several coils of canvas hose heaped around, along with several empty brewskie cans. Somewhere in Chesuncook there is a church—we had seen the steeple spearing through the forest canopy from the lake—and though we look for it on the way out, we don't see it, only raw road and miles and miles of trees.

For the next hour and a half we drive south on the worst road I've seen in the North Country. What a relief to reach the Golden Road, which we find has been newly graded. We turn east toward Millinocket, and sure enough it soon starts raining, then pouring, and the fine gray dust of the Golden Road turns to a fine clay slurry. The tires splatter onward, coating everything: car, trailer, canoes, and all the gear. We transport several buckets of the stuff back to Blue Hill, and I spend the next two days washing everything off with the hose.

Big Reed Pond—Old Growth and Blueback Trout

I've wanted to see Big Reed for a long time. More than twenty years ago a friend said, "Check out Big Reed" during a conversation about old growth forest in Maine. It's a five thousand acre forest preserve held by The Nature Conservancy, and it's never seen an ax. It's also not an easy place to get to. There are no signs, maps, or tourist information helping you get to Big Reed, and that's the way it should be. You can find Big Reed Pond in the *Maine Atlas and Gazetteer*, but then what? There are no boundaries drawn, no access described. It seems like finding Big Reed you are on your own.

I thought the time had come two years ago when Holly and I rented a cabin on Chandler Pond. Big Reed was only a few miles away and, for sure, we'd be able to explore the forest on a day hike. Leading up to our trip, the November days were sunny and sweet with fall, but the day before we left a nor'easter blew in and dumped eight inches of snow on northern Maine. Temperatures dropped to the single numbers, and gale winds flew out of Canada. We decided to put Big Reed on hold.

Months later, browsing Maine sporting camps on the Internet, I clicked on Outpost Cabins at the Bradford Camps website. Up came a log cabin fishing camp on Big Reed Pond. There was something special, a comfortable place to stay in a remote tract of old growth forest. In the fall of 2011, I reserved the cabin for several days in the last week of October. There were a few snow flurries in the forecast, but for most of the time the outlook was sun and temperatures in the 40s.

A few miles outside of Millinocket on the Golden Road, a bloody moose femur lies in the middle of the road. It's one of those signs you're in the North Country—like the image of Katahdin, or the view of the West Branch from the Telos Road. It's a landscape that gets your blood going, the Maine woods. On the Telos Road a small pickup approaches from the north. The driver's head is in shadow, but his fore and middle finger flip a cigarette greeting as we pass. A Plexiglas bug screen above the truck's grill says DILLIGAFF (Do I Look like I Give a Flying Fuck?) in black decals. Next comes a dump truck hauling an excavator so wide it looks like it's going to spill over the sides of the trailer. Right behind is another rig hauling a bulldozer. Both drivers lift a finger. A twelve inch birch log lies in the road. A mile later a large maple straddles the road. It's good to be back north.

North Maine Woods manages checkpoints to control access to the woods, and for half the year collect road and camping fees from people like myself. Telos Gate is one of half a dozen—it overlooks long straightaway on the Telos Road, and a sign instructs drivers to pull over and stop.

"Are you Tod?" asks the lady clerk behind the computer when I walk in.

"How'd you know that?"

She nods at my car parked just outside.

"You've been here before. How many nights?"

"Four."

She enters the information into the computer. "Twenty dollars. Have a nice stay." It's nice being greeted by a real person. Recently North Woods has automated some of the more remote gates because it's cheaper than paying someone. At an unmanned gate you phone in and talk to a controller in Ashland, and after arranging payment, the controller opens the gate for you. Video cameras record the transaction. Wilderness meets the digital age.

Big Reed's isolation is one of its attractions and also one of its challenges. Bradford Camps will fly you in from Munsungan Lake, or there's the way I'm going—a mile hike from the car to the pond, then a canoe paddle across the pond to the cabin. Burdened with my usual abundance of gear, I am resigned to making two trips, which turns a one-mile hike into a three-mile hike. That's OK. There's no hurry, and I can use the exercise. The woods have a way of reducing life to essentials or essences. There isn't anything I have to do but be here.

The trail to the pond starts three miles off the Pinkham Road and traverses the north slope of a hardwood ridge mostly populated with beech. Thousands of head-high saplings are colonizing the ground under the forest canopy, and the breeze flutters the dry beech leaves hanging over the trail which is vague and lacks the depression of well traveled paths. In places it's hard to follow. With the sapling leaves fluttering in my face and the ground covered with leaves, I walk a trail of four dimensions, which is just the kind of immersion I am looking for. At its best, the forest is a salve that sinks into the soul.

Halfway to the pond a small plane flies over the ridge, banks hard to the left, drops eerily down behind the trees, and disappears. I know it's Igor, the owner of Bradford Camps, who said he'd come over to check on me. The last quarter mile of trail slopes down to the spongy shore of Big Reed. Cedar trees hang over the water, the ground is a carpet of moss. Two aluminum canoes rest bottom-up on a couple of logs, and a chilly breeze off the pond blows right at me. There is no plane in sight. A Nature Conservancy sign commemorates the efforts of Stephen Wheatland, 1897-1987, a long-time land agent for the Pingree family, whose vision and resistance to harvesting pressure resulted in the preservation of this tract of old growth forest. I thank Mr. Wheatland for his vision and load gear into a canoe. It's probably intentional that there is no information about where the cabin is, but it can't be that hard to find an airplane on a small pond, and after a few minutes paddling, the plane comes into view in a cove on the south shore.

I find Igor inside the cabin tidying up. He gives me the rundown on the gas stove, the gas lights, the closing up list, and five minutes later he's setting off and "getting out of my hair."

"How long are you going to stay?" he asks. There's a minimum five night rate for the cabin.

"Until Sunday, probably."

"You're a lucky guy, I'll say that. You're a lucky guy." A minute later the plane's engine coughs to a start, and Igor taxis downwind, the red tail light blinking against the dark sward of forest enveloping the little pond. A couple of minutes later Igor lifts off, circles the pond one time, and disappears over the east ridge. As the airplane sounds fade away the forest fills in—the wind sieving the trees, the pond's wavelets splashing on the rocks.

I get a fire going and look around at my home for the next few days. The cabin appears to be twelve feet by sixteen feet, and the only door opens onto a six-foot-deep porch on the water. Firewood is stacked on either side of the porch. A dozen cooking grills hang off nails, a poster of Maine's cold water fish is thumb tacked to the door, a thermometer hangs off a nail, a fire ax and a pry bar lean on the wall. Inside there's a box-type wood stove just inside the door, and a double stainless sink sits in an eight-foot wood grain post-form counter, which is quite a grand kitchen for a North Woods cabin. There's an apartment sized gas stove, metal wall cabinets, and two five-gallon jugs of drinking water. There are three single beds, one single and one bunk bed, and a dining table, on which sit a cribbage board and a couple decks of cards. There's a guest log with entries going back ten years and the pages falling out. In no time the fire drives the chill out, and I'm opening the door to cool off.

It only takes a few minutes to move in. Line the food up right on the counter—the bag of dates, the bag of almonds, teabags, coffee, several baked potatoes, two cans of beans, two loaves of bread. The chicken, hamburg, eggs, bacon, Jarlsberg cheese, and apples stay out on the porch in a big pot. This time of year Mother Nature provides the refrigeration.

My forty-year-old down sleeping bag still shows some loft. It's lost a lot of feathers and has had many generations of duct tape patches, but still works for a camp bag. A pillowcase from home receives three old pillows found in a mouse-proof linen box standing between the beds. The linen box is an old wooden freight box. Long ago someone painted the address on the side in black paint: "To the Libby Brothers, by R.R. to Masardis."

Next I arrange all the trip paraphernalia on the table—maps, compass, pens, notebooks, camera, headlamp. There, I'm moved in. Now what? I'm alone miles in the middle of the woods. The soughing wind seems to whisper a foreign language. Suddenly a wave of loneliness overwhelms me. I miss Holly and the cat, and wish Holly was here to share this with me.

I make a cup of tea and sit on the porch to watch the shadows gathering on the pond. Cedar, pine, and spruce surround the dark waters, but high up the flank of Reed Mountain, the setting sun lights a fire in the spruce cones. Above the fir spires, and the spruce, and the gangly boughs of pine, the bare hardwood ridge whistles in the wind. Lower down the mountain, against a spread of moody conifers, a swatch of rusty beech leaves hang on in a flourish. At 5:30 P.M. I fry chicken breasts and warm the baked potatoes on top of the wood stove. By seven

I'm in bed reading the cabin guest book. One man who came in with his two sons to fish for a couple of days remarked it was very annoying when one boy fell out of the upper bunk and landed face down on the floor.

Night in the cabin is unbelievably dark—a black hole kind of dark. It's a supersaturated blackness so dense it floats you, holds you up above the nothingness. There's no window near the bed, nowhere to see the sky, so at 1:00 A.M. when I go out to pee, it's a relief to see the stars. My bare feet leave melt tracks in the frost.

At five I strike a match under the gas lights, and the glow breathes life into the cabin. The four coffee pots would make coffee for thirty people, but I choose a funky old aluminum percolator, and in five minutes the coffee starts spluttering out of a lid that doesn't fit snugly. Out on the porch the sun makes headway in the eastern sky, and slowly the forest casts off the shadows of night. Across the cove the white breasts of mergansers glow on the dark waters.

I think it's a misconception that places like this are quiet. Visitors write in the camp journal that staying here is the experience of a lifetime and express reverence for the pond and the quiet. One was astounded by the silence. I know what they mean, but what they are talking about is the absence of sound originating in human activity. Traffic, piped music, airplanes, human voices, machinery contribute to a background din that overpowers natural sounds and the sounds of our own thoughts. So we come to learn the absence of human sounds is quiet, but if you really listen to the quiet you will hear the pure sounds of nature. A wisp of breeze blows through the trees, and the forest is a woodwind of a million reeds. The pond wavelets sing on the mossy rocks. A red squirrel chits an aria. And if all else falls still and slumbers, there is still the keening between your own ears.

The still pond waters of the early morning beckon, and with coffee in hand I launch the Grumman, careful to keep the paddle away from the rails of the aluminum canoe, lest I send a drum signal announcing I am here to my neighbors in the forest. It reminds me of an airplane, a utilitarian artifact that makes common sense in this remote pond. This canoe will never share the fate of the wood and canvas canoes long abandoned on the shore and returning to the land like rotten logs.

On a small pond like Big Reed, water and woods intermingle around the edges so there is no definite shoreline. Water laps at the tree trunks, and some cedars grow horizontally over the surface, their branches hanging in the water. The hulk of a pine tree lies across a mossy swale where the sun never shines. In a large hollow log resting in the shallows, a cluster of mussel shells glow like pearls under water. They are Eastern Floaters, a delicacy for muskrats, and the log is a muskrat dining room. At the west end of the pond, I float over a cluster of deer bones. Wobbly under the moving water, the bones are spectral runes written on the heart of the forest.

After returning to the cabin, tidying up a bit—sweeping twigs and leaves from the floor and the porch, leaning the ax against the wall just so—I fill a water bottle and set out to walk around to the north side of the pond. There are no trails in the area—though some routes are flagged with tape—the mile long trek to Little Reed is flagged—so overland travel means bushwacking. Sometimes the going is open and easy, but then you can find yourself in a soggy mire battling blow downs and brush. The moose is well served in these forests, and I wouldn't mind a set of moose legs myself.

An old growth forest is a mosaic of trees—standing mature trees, quarter-inch-thick saplings, decaying forest whales redolent with moss and lichen. Diversity. Muck at the pond edge. Every fifty-odd feet a beaver path makes up into the woods far enough for them to find something to cut down and eat. In an old forest like this, the animals' habits are fingerprints on the ground. In some places the game trails are so worn they look like the hiking trails in Baxter Park. These are the centuries-old byways of the moose and the deer, the humans who lived here. But they don't go far. Too soon the trail dissolves, and the walker meets an impasse of huge trunks and branches, a chaos of impenetrable pulp.

Halfway around the pond, I consider the consequences of walking three-quarters of the way around and not being able to cross the beaver pond at the outlet. I don't know what I'll find, but my hips are sore from yesterday's hike in, and I don't want to take the chance of doubling my intended hike, so I turn back for the cabin. The hips flare up after carrying heavy loads—a bad omen no doubt—and I have no desire to encourage hip replacements.

The log cabin is a welcome refuge after an outing. The temperatures outside are in the upper 30s, but inside the cabin is toasty. In this weather it stays comfortable for hours with only a couple of pieces of split cedar laid on top of the coals. I imagine having a few cords of wood on hand and spending a month of deep winter here. That would be a trial of solitude. I had hoped to have the company of loons here but am too late—they have already moved to the coast for the winter. So I sit on the porch and look around. If this were my camp, there would be things to do. Cut firewood, continue repairs to the cabins, clean up a couple of windthrows on the path to the landing. But I have paid for this leisure time. I have bought this time for contemplation.

It is hard to put the solitude into words. In some ways it feels like an aberrant experience, and I wonder what the point of it is. The moment is beautiful, but I make no mistake that this is a temporary solitude, as I want it to be, and is subsidized by the outside world. It is subsidized by the Nature Conservancy which owns the old growth forest. It is subsidized by Igor and Bradford Camps, and by me. It's a Thursday. People are at home working a job, making a living. I am up here experiencing the pond and the woods, and certainly no one is paying me.

The longer I'm here, the more the story of the Big Reed fish rises to the surface. Big Reed Pond is one of only a few Maine ponds that blueback trout call home. But some years ago in the early 1990s, some jerks introduced rainbow smelt to Big Reed, and the non native species' population exploded at the expense of the bluebacks, to the point where a few years ago the trout were down to a handful of fish. Now the smelt are gone and the trout are back, and the story of how it happened is a saga of hope and heart.

The blueback trout, or Arctic Char, live in only fourteen ponds in the United States; all of them are in Maine, and Big Reed is one of them. The bluebacks colonized these ponds fifteen thousand years ago when the glaciers retreated, and salt water flooded the depressed landmass. When the land rebounded, fresh water replaced salt water, and the fish evolved genetically isolated from other blueback populations and their oceanic lineages.

It only took a few years for the smelt to attain dominance. They feasted on the blueback smolts and the smolts of the other native pond species, the brook trout. Biologists were keen on maintaining genetic continuity in Big Reed's ecosystem, and their plan called for raising a new population of blueback and brook trout at commercial hatcheries using eggs milked from Big Reed fish. So complete was the smelt's invasion that when Maine's Inland Fisheries and Wildlife (IFW) began reclamation in 2007, over a three-year period only a dozen bluebacks were taken from Big Reed. The first year in captivity, survival rates of the young fish were negligible, but the second and third years were successful. In 2009 four thousand blueback embryos survived at the Frenchville Hatchery, and while the smolts grew into sturdy yearlings, the scientists fine-tuned a plan to take out Big Reed's uninvited guests, the rainbow smelt and another invader, the white sucker.

It took three years of planning to be ready for the application of the piscicide rotenone. The poison would wipe the pond slate clean of anything with gills, an unusual ecological status, so the way would be clear to reintroduce to the pond the fish that had been raised in the hatcheries. In October 2010 two Army Black Hawk helicopters lifted over six tons of rotenone from a road site a few miles away to the pond, and the eventual application of the poison yielded thousands of rainbow smelt, white suckers, and creek chubs. It yielded no bluebacks and only forty brook trout, several of which were revived in clean water.

At this point, in the words of Frank Frost, the lead biologist from IFW, Big Reed was poised for a new start. It had a clean ecological slate. In fact it was in an unnatural condition that had never before existed. During the winter of 2010-2011, for the first time ever no fish lived under the ice. Then, in June 2011, not long after ice out, the team released three hundred char and five hundred and fifty brook trout. In October they released two hundred char and six hundred brook trout. The thirteen mergansers diving in the calm shallows of the northwest cove are feeding on the trout fry spawned from the stocked fish. The pond has been cleansed and is alive again with a pure lineage that reaches back to the Ice Age.

The reclamation of Big Reed is a wonderful story. It is also a cautionary tale. The problem resulted in the first place from human selfishness and ignorance—two traits we harbor in abundance. Though Big Reed was a challenge because of its remote location, its manageable scale and isolation from other ecosystems also made the reclamation possible. Most ecological imbalances are not so easily reversed. It reminds us of man's boundless capacity to screw things up, and it reminds us of the capacity of human resources and ingenuity to do good in the world.

When I sit on the porch and watch the trout-rising circles blossom across the cove in the black mirror of water, everything feels so fragile. Since I got here, the big indifferent west wind has sheared the trees up on Reed Mountain, winked silver ripples on the pond. Big Reed is a mote of an island anchored in the sea of industry and greed, acquisition and profit. I am not talking about the industrial forest on the other side of the hill—I am talking about the world of seven billion people seething at the breasts of the earth. The solitude at Big Reed is as frail as we are.

A Last Word for Wilderness

It seems to me that as human beings we create too much of our reality, or call it our environment, by a seat- of- the- pants necessity. Our economic and political institutions either do not anticipate, or choose to ignore, warnings of detrimental behavior that diminish health and well being for the planetary biome. The result is we end up designing our future in the rear view mirror, trying to correct our mistakes as we go along. It's not a great way to do it, but perhaps we're learning a better way.

The Maine Woods offers up a pretty good metaphor for the complex tensions characterizing modern society. Two centuries ago the Maine Woods were virtually given away to well connected individuals who initiated a forest products industry that evolves to this day. Timber has been the lifeblood of the north, though jobs and livelihood are in decline due to mechanization and changing markets. Growing urban populations, declining traditional industries, and the presence of real estate investment companies now bring great pressure on the integrity of the Maine Woods. The existing network of roads that provide access to pond, lake, river and stream waterfronts and camp lots are enough to make a real estate man drool.

Still, even though the Woods are fragmented by a patchwork of ownership, bisected by thousands of miles of roads, Maine's northern forest is substantially undeveloped at this time. In the state controlled Allagash Wilderness Waterway, and Baxter State Park we have two stunning examples of conservation success, and there are others. The Nature Conservancy and the Appalachian Mountain Club hold easements or own outright thousands of acres. There is yet opportunity for reunification.

The bottom line is when we conserve landscape we conserve the human spirit. We may not always be aware that's what's happening, but I believe it's true. That's why I go into the woods, and that's why all the places in this book are important. When my mother was able to walk away from her hospital bed, the thing she wanted most was to experience some nature around her. Like food and shelter and clothing, it's essential to our survival.

www.ingramcontent.com/pod-product-compliance
Lightning Source LLC
Chambersburg PA
CBHW070538290526
45790CB00002B/547